David M. McCormick

Short-Term Pastoral Counseling

-A GUIDE-

SHORT-TERM PASTORAL COUNSELING

-A GUIDE-

Brian H. Childs

Abingdon Press

Nashville

Short-term Pastoral Counseling: A Guide

Copyright © 1990 by Abingdon Press

All rights reserved.

This book is printed on acid-free paper.

Library of Congress Cataloging-in-Publication Data

Childs, Brian H., 1947–
    Short-term pastoral counseling : a guide / Brian H. Childs.
      p. cm.
    ISBN 0-687-38432-X (alk. paper)
    1. Pastoral counseling. 2. Psychotherapy, Brief. I. Title.
BV4012.2.C45 1990
253.2—dc20   90-34736
                                         CIP

MANUFACTURED IN THE UNITED STATES OF AMERICA

to the memory of
Father George Christulides

Contents

Introduction

This book is intended for three primary audiences. First is the parish pastor who is not only interested in counseling but who finds it difficult if not impossible to go about the daily work of parish ministry without being confronted with requests for counseling, however disguised those requests may be. Most pastors do not experience a lack of counseling opportunities; rather two other factors militate against the pastor engaging in pastoral counseling in the parish. The first problem is the issue of time: there is so little of it to devote to the time-consuming job of responsible pastoral counseling. The second dilemma is found in the general pastor who often has very little training other than basic pastoral care education and training. Then follows a lack of confidence in doing good and responsible pastoral counseling in the parish setting. This book shall respond to these two common perceptions of the counseling task by many parish pastors. While both perceptions have validity, it is inaccurate to rule out the pastor's ability to perform disciplined pastoral counseling. This book will offer the parish generalist a structure to enable him or her to manage better his or her pastoral counseling time as well as have more control over the process of the counseling itself.

The second intended audience is the seminarian who is interested in better preparation for his or her future parish work and the ministry of pastoral care and counseling. This seminarian is probably a senior with a basic course in pastoral care, and possibly a course or two in advanced pastoral care and counseling or pastoral theology, or possibly a basic quarter of CPE. This seminarian is probably already aware of the pressures of time and confidence that plague the well-established parish pastor. He or she is convinced that some approach should be considered to help confront the problems before they actually begin.

The third audience is the advanced student in pastoral counseling or established specialists in pastoral counseling. While these people may judge some of the material in this book elementary, it is my hope that they will find some value in the method I propose, especially in the diagnostic approach and flow of a short-term counseling process. Certainly many of these pastoral care specialists may find something to ponder in considering a short-term approach, especially if they are more used to a long-term, non-problem-solving form of counseling or psychotherapy.

All three audiences are offered a particularly theological approach to understanding the pastoral counseling context no matter if they are specialists, in training, or practicing in a parish setting. Time is a basic issue in what it is to be human. As finite creatures we only have so much of it. As fallible creatures we attempt to flee from the responsibility that is inherent in the limitation of our time. As hopeful creatures we long for the end of troubling time. Our use and understanding of time tells us much about ourselves, and (in terms of a theological anthropology) our understanding of time may give us some sense of a normative vision of how God intends us to be in light of our limitations and freedom. This book not only offers a way for pastoral counseling to be done parsimoniously and with some assurance of control on the part of the counselor, but it also points the way for the pastor to be theologian as well as counselor and manager.

While this book is intended .as an easy-to-follow manual for investigating and performing time-limited, problem-solving counseling in the parish setting, much can be learned from good books on the subject of counseling which are not just of a theoretical nature but also of a practical nature. Rollo May's *The Art of Counseling* and Seward Hiltner's *Pastoral Counseling* are good examples of counseling manuals which offer theory and practical and technical advice. Counseling, however, should also be learned through its practice and the disciplined reflection upon that practice. A person's ability to learn about the counseling process is enhanced by ongoing counseling under the careful supervision of peers and/or supervisors, the latter being understood as more advanced in their counseling training and experience. As intensely private and intimate as counseling can be between the counselor and the counselee, it is irresponsible for the pastor not to have some kind of public accountability for the ethical and competent practice of pastoral counseling. Competent, confidential, and ethical supervision either with peers or singly with a specialist is essential. I assume, therefore, that if time-limited pastoral coun-seling is attempted, and this book is used as a basis for this practice, then it is used in concert with some form of responsible supervision and accountability. The issue of consultation and supervision is fully discussed in chapter 4.

This book proceeds first from a pastoral and theological

assessment of the issue of time. It then proceeds to define time-limited counseling by borrowing not only from my own experience in time-limited counseling but also from the rather expansive literature in psychiatry and psychology on the subject of time-limited therapy. The book then offers a structure for performing time-limited counseling with details for diagnosis, counselee selection, and the structural process of a ten-session time-limited counseling program. Case examples are given throughout each of the chapters. The case materials are composites from my own clinical work as well as that of some of my students. Identities have been changed to protect confidentiality. The book concludes with further pastoral theological reflections.

The impetus for this book came from a course on parish pastoral counseling taught at Princeton Theological Seminary in 1983. At that time I was not so interested in the particular qualities of an actual time-limited counseling contract as I was for helping minimally trained seminary students who were anticipating parish work and learning something about counseling. Over the years this course has developed into a more clearly defined look at time-limited counseling within the parish setting. I have also benefited from the input of students in various degree programs at three other seminaries. Many thanks are due to students not only at Princeton, but also to students who have been enrolled in the M.Div. programs at Moravian Theological Seminary and Columbia Theological Seminary; in the Th.M. program at Princeton, New Brunswick Theological Seminary, and Columbia; and D.Min. and STD students at Columbia, and the Candler School of Theology of Emory University. Not all of these students have been enthusiastic about the approach that I am proposing.

Nearly all of them have been very helpful, however, in their criticism and have helped me refine my approach.

I must also give credit for the help I have received from colleagues in formulating this book. John Patton, as always, has been a faithful and critical friend and senior colleague. It was John who first suggested to me that time-limited pastoral counseling just may be an oxymoron. I don't believe that is the case and so we disagree. It is my hope that my argument is clear, though it may not always be convincing to all. I also want to express my gratitude to Jasper N. Keith, another of my senior colleagues at Columbia. Jap has given me the space to develop my skills as a teacher and has given me the encouragement to continue my vocation of scholarship and ministry. Ann Titshaw, my secretary, has been patient in spite of my occasional petulance and in spite of being a manager of an office that houses John, Jap, and myself with all the clutter that results from our teaching, writing, counseling, and organizing. It is amazing how much she does with such grace and ease. I also wish to thank the Dean and Vice President of Academic Affairs at Columbia, Glenn R. Bucher, and his recent predecessor Oscar Hussel for their support.

I have learned and will continue to learn about the human condition from my relationship with my pastoral counseling clients. Of course my family has been a lasting resource of patience as I completed the manuscript. Sandy, Caitlin, and Alexander have my eternal thanks. I also want to thank Dr. Paul Franklyn, professional books editor, and Cheryl Balthrop of Abingdon Press for their help in the final preparation of the manuscript.

Several of the authors that I have quoted from do not use inclusive language. The reasons for this are mostly due to the historical era and social customs in regard to language in which these authors did their work. Rather than alter any quotation that I have used in order to be inclusive or mark non-inclusive language with the notation of *sic* I have let their language be their own. In many ways I have found the non-inclusive use of language in these quotations to be shocking to my own sensitivities, and I hope it will be to those of the reader as well. For this reason, leaving them may itself prove instructive. In my own use of language I have been sensitive to the important issue of inclusiveness.

Finally this book is dedicated to the memory of Father George Christulides late of St. Vasilios Greek Orthodox Church in Peabody and Holy Cross Greek Orthodox Seminary in Brookline. George was a Ph.D. student of mine at Princeton and Trinity Counseling Service in Princeton. I first began to think about the usefulness and importance of time-limited counseling with George and a couple of other doctrinal students, Brad Binau and Jeff Patton. George and his peers were very helpful in those early days. George was also a friend and colleague, and though geographical distance made our meetings less frequent over the last couple of years, our mutual respect and affection had continued to thrive. His early death is a loss not only to the Greek Orthodox Church but also to pastoral theology in general. His loss to his wife, Lia, and his young daughter, Thespina Maria, is indescribable. It is to him that this essay on the limitation of our time on earth and our call to the ministry of counseling is dedicated.

1

The Context of Parish Counseling

The pastor's counseling ministry is found in the context of pastoral identity, pastoral initiative, and the limitation of time. Pastors are more than preachers and organizers. They also are counselors and theologians. It is within this context that pastors can fulfill their ministry and be theologically reflective and responsible in their task.

Theological education is now criticized on several fronts. Generally theological education has too readily adopted the professional model of education for clergy at the expense of a more attitudinal approach.[1] Most of the critics argue that the professional model stresses too much the technical ability of the minister over and against that of the laity at the expense of what has been called the distinctive theological and sacramental dimensions of ministry. In pastoral care and pastoral counseling, the professional model, so the argument goes, separates the minister from his or her counselee and therefore truncates what should be an intensely personal encounter. According to Alastair V. Campbell, "To offer oneself as an accredited helper is to impose limits upon the character of the relationship, to keep oneself apart in order to concentrate on the need of the other and to define the duration and depth of the encounter solely according to what the other requires in order to be helped. But is this also the true character of pastoral care as the increase of love of God and neighbor?"[2]

There are serious problems that can arise when the pastor does identify his or her caring and counseling with the office model (fee for service) that is offered by psychotherapy. This is the model that Campbell fears may become normative for all of pastoral care. The model of a pastoral counselor imitating the psychoanalyst who is passive, save for timed interpretations, is one that sets apart the helper from the moral and theological struggles in which both the counselor and the counselee should be involved. The model of the pastoral specialist as expert and the counselee as passive and in need precludes mutuality, according to Campbell, and this is contrary to Christian relatedness and the doctrine of the priesthood of all believers.[3]

While there is considerable power and passion in the arguments that are made by pastoral counseling's critics, they are far too broadly made and may have more rhetorical force than practical value. While there is no question that the pastor who avoids being involved in the day-to-day life of his or her parishioners by remaining office-bound sacrifices a valuable part of ministry, that alone does not obviate the place of personal and private counseling in the pastoral study. People can respond to a pastor's sermons, social activity, and presence with a desire for personal counseling concerning relationship problems. To deny this aspect of ministry or to relegate it solely to the referral of persons to secular counselors is to limit a traditionally important part of the shepherding function of ministry.

Many arguments against the counseling model as a

part of ministry strike me as naive about counseling itself. Many of the critics seem to have the so-called classical long-term psychoanalytic process as their model for all of pastoral counseling. I do not know of a single pastor—or even a full-time pastoral counselor—who does counseling, who is also a psychoanalyst, remains passive with his or her client (with no eye contact), uses a couch, and limits his or her verbal interaction during the first of what could be four or five years of sessions three times a week. In fact there are very few classical analysts practicing, save for a few in major cities such as New York and Chicago. Pastoral psychotherapy is active and interactive; transference and countertransference—that is, feelings about the counselor and the counselor's own feelings—are important from the beginning; and contact with the client in normal social and ecclesiastical settings is not uncommon.

Finally, so the critical argument goes, pastoral counseling has been called into question because it has seemingly turned its back on a tradition that predates, by several millennia, the advent of modern psychotherapy. While there is much to be learned from the tradition and from the tradition's interpreters, this argument strikes me as being antiquarian at worst and naive at best. To say that pastoral care prior to the advent of modern psychology was devoid of a psychological understanding of humankind is arrogant and plainly false.[4] Additionally, particularly from a Reformed Protestant point of view, Christian life cannot be lived outside of culture. Our vocation as Christians is to live in the world and care for all of creation and not just that which we attempt to create for ourselves. There is no inherent danger in Christian faith and action availing itself of the human sciences, including counseling theory and techniques.

The Background of Pastoral Counseling

Pastoral counseling and pastoral care are not twentieth-century inventions. Of course the techniques and the occasions for pastoral care and counseling in this century are in many ways unique to this era, but the care or cure of souls has been a province of the church, and of religions in general, from the beginnings of recorded history.[5] Most recently E. Brooks Holifield has argued that in North America over the past four hundred years pastoral care and counseling has had a variety of operating theories that have guided pastors and lay ministers alike in their duties of counseling.[6] These theories have incorporated rationalistic and emotional appeals to those who have been ministered to by ministers who have self-consciously systematic approaches to their work. It would be a condescending and chauvinistic mistake to assume, for instance, that some early pre-revolutionary pastors had no notion of a psychology of humans. Jonathan Edwards' *Treatise Concerning Religious Affections* comes immediately to mind as a systematic psychology that guided much pastoral care.[7]

Of course it is true that most of what could be called pastoral counseling before the current century would seem unrecognizable to most of us. Prior to the current century, clinical counseling in any way similar to modern forms was basically non-existent in either secular or pastoral work. With the interest in Freudian personality theory and clinical technique, particularly in America, that began shortly after Freud's visit to Clark University in 1909, the approach to human problems began to become more and more "psychotherapeutic" and less observational and custodial. Clinical therapy was slow to develop and often in competition with the politically powerful medical profession. People such as Anton Boisen, Helen Flanders Dunbar, Seward Hiltner, Carol Wise, and Wayne Oates pioneered the clinical movement in both theological education and the work of the minister. These pioneers, among others, not only interpreted the advances and findings of modern psychology and psychiatry but also illustrated the value of these new fields for pastoral work.[8] It was not until the mid-point of the current century that psychotherapy as we know it came to be of value to the pastor. Before this time psychological treatment was limited either to grossly disturbed people or to the wealthy who could afford a lengthy and often self-indulgent psychoanalysis. For a variety of reasons, many of them pragmatic, newer forms of therapy were developed after the end of World War II. These therapies were designed for the treatment of more common and less crippling problems such as marital and family problems, substance abuse, depression, and compulsive behavior. Here again, many practical theologians interpreted these developments to the church and began to promote certain adaptations for pastoral use.[9]

Why People Go to Pastors

Though there are a plethora of mental health practitioners available to most people, particularly those who live in or near the large metropolitan areas, people still go to pastors. Just as important, pastors have an *entre* to people that most mental health professionals do not have.

Masters and Johnson tell us that 70 percent of all the people who consulted their foundation had at one time or another also consulted a minister about their problem. While I think this is a surprisingly high percentage of people seeking help from ministers with a potentially delicate set of problems, it certainly underscores a point. People go to pastors for help. While often people will come to a pastor with nothing more in mind than "chatting," it will become more and more clear to the pastor with some counseling experience that there is often a matrix of conflicts and problems that the person brings along with the desire "just to talk." Reactive depressions over the loss of a job, the loss of loved ones, children leaving home (or returning home) are very commonly heard complaints in the pastor's study. Marital problems, substance abuse, problems with children, economic stress, and most recently, anxiety concerning nuclear holocaust are often brought to the attention of the pastor.

Why people go to pastors when they perceive themselves to have problems too heavy for them to carry alone is an interesting question. Certainly the notion that pastors are compassionate and caring people able to listen is an earned one. That pastors are known more and more to have an interest in counseling and problem solving is a growing recognition. I suspect that many a pastor telegraphs his or her willingness to be with people in need through the sermon on Sunday morning and his or her presence in the hospital on a regular basis. Of course, word of mouth, probably the most reliable basis for at least talking to the pastor, is a referral source appreciated both by the religious as well as the secular professional.

Pastors can also go to people. Unlike any other professional, the minister can solicit his or her services to those that are seen to be in need. This is the most liberating and potentially dangerous aspect of pastoral work. It is liberating in that it allows pastors to work unhindered by the common social pressure to ignore the destitute, the sick, the hungry, and the disturbed. The pastor, like the Samaritan, does not expect a *quid pro quo* for his or her work (though emotionally that may not always be the case). Service is given as a witness of the church. Certainly if the troubled person or persons are members of the church of which the pastor is the shepherd, then unsolicited intervention, while it may be rejected, is expected.

The Goals of Pastoral Counseling

Pastoral counseling has two primary goals. The first is to enable persons to help themselves. This does not mean that the goal of pastoral counseling is to make people totally self-sufficient and individualistic, as if that were really possible or desirable. One sign of being able to take care of oneself is to take responsibility for the self by living in a community and taking advantage of its resources as well as contributing to them. The rugged individualist (most often a man in our culture) who declares that asking for help is a sign of weakness is just as much at fault as the chronic seeker of help and support.

The pastor is in a unique position to make both individual and systemic evaluations of what creates the problem and what resources are available. The pastor who is trained in general pastoral work and is current in his or her study of theology offers a perspective not shared with many secular counselors. The pastor is interested both in the dynamics of the individual and in representing a community of resources. The pastor, then, can identify both social and individual concerns and should be capable of correlating the two.

The second goal of pastoral counseling is to allow the counseling experience to be a resource for a fuller and richer theological understanding of human nature. Pastoral counseling as a ministry of the church must therefore contribute to the church's understanding of itself, its mission, and the world in which it lives. Seward Hiltner defines well the theological contribution that pastoral counseling can make in his *Preface to Pastoral Theology*.[10] Material that is collected in the pastor's shepherding function can illuminate our understanding of common words of faith (such as God, humanity, sin, salvation) and also illustrate humankind's reaction to God and God's activity through Christ.[11]

Pastoral care contributes to the task of constructive theology. John Patton's *Is Human Forgiveness Possible?* makes the observation that the various notions of the atonement are inadequate in understanding the realized experience of forgiveness.[12] The atonement and the doctrinal variations of forgiveness necessarily imply some kind of hierarchy: a sinless God forgiving errant creatures. When this is applied to the process among creatures (following the sixth petition of the Lord's Prayer) it becomes problematical. There seems implied a human hierarchy with some kind of qualitative and quantitative level of sinfulness between the wronged and the wrongdoer. Through an investigation of the history of the doctrine of forgiveness and with help from behavioral sciences dealing with object relations theory and shame theory, Patton concludes that forgiveness is not something that one does (one to another, right over wrong) but is something that one discovers. One forgives because one finds that there is no room to forgive at all. We are all more like the wrongdoer than we are different.

Harry Emerson Fosdick also used his counseling as material for understanding a humanity struggling with an understanding of faith. Fosdick prepared for his sermons not only with biblical exegesis but with detailed reflection on counseling that he performed throughout the week. His understanding of tradition went hand in hand with his understanding of creatureliness.

Achieving the Goals

Pastoral counseling—whether as part of a general practice of ministry or the primary focus of a specialized ministry—has two goals. The healing goal entails diagnostic, social, and rehabilitative complexities. The second goal is the constructive task of theological understanding. Pastoral counseling is applied theology. Pastoral counseling is also part of the research arm of constructive theology. The pastoral counselor is a minister and a theologian. When the two are separated, only mischief can occur: either technical preoccupation without any unifying theoretical basis for activity or intellectual abstraction alien to the vicissitudes of life and faith.

In order to fulfill these two goals the pastor needs to have at a minimum an interest in the current issues of theology, as well as a grasp of the history of the Christian tradition and his or her own denominational tradition. The pastor who is lucky enough to work in close proximity to a seminary with a continuing education program can, with some discipline, keep up with current theological thinking. In addition there are several journals that can be read and digested. *Theology Today, Interpretation, Pastoral Psychology,* and the *Journal of Pastoral Care* are valuable and useful journals that will help the pastor be aware, through articles and book reviews, of the current theological climate.

Another valuable way of keeping up with theological thinking for those not near a major theological school is to form reading groups with other pastors in the area. Books can be read and discussed—a few chapters at a time—over a brown bag lunch or morning coffee. My own experience is that pastors have a difficult time making such a time sacrosanct, but once established, the fellowship and learning become more valuable than was ever imagined.

Another way of achieving the goals of pastoral counseling is to have some basic working knowledge of a dynamic personality theory and counseling techniques that are based on that theory. Here, as with continued theological study, the pastor can use community resources that may be at hand. Theological seminaries, study groups, and the important supervision group are helpful resources.

By using the term *dynamic* I am of course referring to the theories of personality that have some heritage with psychoanalysis, as developed by Sigmund Freud. There have been many revisions of Freudian thought, each falling under the definition of dynamic psychology.[13] Essentially, dynamic theory views the personality and its development as occurring in a sphere of conflict. The needs and desires of the person are continually being confronted with resistances, inhibitions, and prohibitions (both of a physical and psychological nature) and these affect the mode of living of the individual as he or she attempts to adapt to these conflicts. Life, according to this general theory, is a continual process of maneuvering, avoiding, and conquering those obstacles perceived to be in the way of satisfying needs and desires. Trouble occurs when the adaptation to the perceived obstacles also inhibits the day-to-day ability of the person to work and be in close personal relationships.

Hiltner in *Pastoral Counseling* has outlined four major points of dynamic psychology that are particularly helpful in the work of the pastoral counselor. First, all conduct has meaning. By this he means that no behavior is simply capricious.

Instead of saying that a pastor should not be shocked or surprised by anything that comes to light, we may better say that if he knows all conduct has meaning, however bizarre it may appear on the surface, the mere appearance of the bizarre, whether we understand its meaning or not, cannot shock or surprise us. For we take it for granted there is meaning there.[14]

Second, the meaning of all conduct is understood only if we look at both the conscious awareness and at the deeper levels that influence personality that may not always be conscious. Hiltner offers a short verbatim account that illustrates this process.

A student comes to his pastor for a scheduled counseling appointment. On his way he notices that the library is closed and notes it without any particular emphasis. He then enters the pastor's study with a whistle and a jump in his gait.

Student: I wonder why I had that feeling [of happiness]. I can't think of anything that happened while I was coming over here, and I remember I didn't feel that way when I left home.

Pastor: You came the shortest way?

Student: No, I came around past the library. That's the only thing I can remember—that the library was closed. I don't know why; I thought it was open today.

Pastor: Did anything go across your mind when you noted the library was closed?

Student: Why, yes, it did. It just flashed in my mind and was gone. I thought to myself: "Good, now no one can get any books out today and get ahead of me in my studies." Gee, and that made me happy.

Pastor: It looks as though it took the disadvantage of others to produce happiness in you. Maybe we'd better look at that.

Student: I guess we'd better.[15]

Third, personality grows through the constructive handling of conflict and not by the absence of conflict.[16]

Personality development is a process that finds the person facing conflicts, resolving them and achieving some kind of psychic equilibrium, and then facing disequilibrium when other and possibly more complex situations arise. The development of social ability in the child is a way of illustrating this point. The child's first social world is that of the relationship with parents and possibly siblings. While there are conflicts that the child must deal with within this social world, the ones that the child must face as he or she goes off to school or to the playground with other non-family members are ever more complicated. Adequate social development depends upon the child's ability to handle the conflict of these larger societies present in opposition to the rules of behavior found in the home.

Finally, Hiltner observes that the human personality is always more than those aspects that are consciously recognized.[17] Pastoral counselors will recognize the multiplicity of personality as it attempts to deal with inevitable conflict. "The most vital question about a person always is: In what fundamental direction is he moving? Is it compromise, concealment, fixation, projection; or is it, however small the achievement be in a quantitative sense, in the direction of growth through constructive dealing with conflict?"[18]

The reader will notice that Hiltner's understanding of dynamic personality development chronicles both internal and external conflict. Humans are social animals, and there are as many, if not more, conflicts inherent in being social as there are in conflicted internal desires and needs. Very early in infancy the child learns about social conflicts and the avoidance of them. Sometimes the measures that a child will develop to avoid social anxiety within the home are carried on in later life where they may or may not be adequate to the task. As I have mentioned above, the school is not the home. Defensive postures or other ways of behaving socially, while they may be good for one place, may not be so good in another. It is in the conflict of personally developed patterns of behavior with societal patterns of behavior that most people find themselves in trouble and, at times, seek help.

While the above outline of dynamic personality theory is no more than a surface description, the following chapters will build on these four aspects. In sum, personality is developed within the conflict of the needs and desires of the individual in a social environment with other social creatures who also process needs and desires. Some of our needs and desires are conscious while others are unconscious. Personality consists of fulfilling needs and desires within a social context; and these desires, both conscious and unconscious, are acted out through behavior. Trouble occurs when unconscious needs and desires are acted out behaviorally, or when social behaviors are adequate in one social context but not in another.

The Problem of Time

Time is another important element in the pastor's approach to pastoral counseling. Pastors in the local parish are very busy people with many duties to perform, including study. Even if a pastor is called to a particular parish to be involved in pastoral care and counseling, time can soon become in short supply. Good and disciplined counseling takes more time than that used in the direct counseling itself. A pastor also needs to review process notes, get supervision, and plan subsequent meetings with the counselee. All of this takes time. At the same time, counseling requests keep mounting and this puts the pastor, especially the one who enjoys counseling, in a difficult spot. Certainly, the pastor's development of adequate referral resources is one way to take care of the requests for counseling. Another solution, when appropriate, is the development of group sessions that center upon themes such as single person concerns, single parenting, and couples groups. Of course group work demands its own skills, and individual people still will request private counseling.

Psychiatric clinics and counseling agencies around the country also are confronted with time problems. Waiting lists have continued to grow, and more and more therapists have full practices and are closed to new clients. During the 1960s one solution to this problem was developed: time-limited counseling. Some clinicians found that treatment that was focused and limited in duration was quite successful in helping people to do problem solving and achieve certain clearly articulated goals. Time-limited therapy has been defined as anywhere from six to twenty or thirty sessions of fifty minutes per session. In order to make it truly time-limited, there is no renegotiation for new contracts for additional counseling with the same counselor. Time-limited therapy is also rather task oriented and generally focuses upon what I shall call the Focal Relational Problem. I am referring to the one problem that the counselee has described as recurring so often that emotional and social difficulties arise. Generally these types of problems revolve around relationships or are at least seen as arising out of repeated failed or unsatisfying relationships. Such issues as depression, grief, obsessionalism, and only occasionally alcohol abuse can be seen most clearly within the context of failed or unsatisfying relationships. The problem is then addressed by the counselor both through the client's own re-enacting of the problem in the day-to-day activities that are reported in counseling, and in the development of the problem as it is enacted within the counseling process between the counselee and the counselor.

While time-limited counseling has been practiced and taught for at least two decades, surprisingly very few of its major theorists have been interested in what time means to both the counselor and counselee, with the exception of its effect on scheduling. Time and its inherent limitations have a more profound meaning.

In his work *Time-Limited Psychotherapy*, Mann argues that "all short forms of psychotherapy, whether their practitioners know it or not, revive the horror of time."[19] The basic conflict that people face when confronted with time limitation is the conflict between infantile timelessness and the reality of inevitable loss. Children up to adolescence have a very limited consciousness of time. For them time is mostly a framework in which to perform functions such as sleeping, eating, and going to the toilet. In adolescence time becomes more and more acute. "Adolescents become sorely conflicted because they know that there is limited time available for making certain life decisions, so that the characteristic ambivalence at this developmental period is heightened by preoccupations with time."[20] The yearning for the timelessness of youth when an adult faces important decisions are hallmarks of human ambivalence and ambiguity.

All these situations constitute clearcut evidence for the presence of a sense of timelessness residing in the unconscious of all humans. An even more remarkable expression of it is the fact that no person *feels* himself to be growing old. In the presence of good health, we do not experience the advance of old age. We do perceive the effects of the aging process and we are aware *inwardly* of having grown older. The pursuit of timelessness, of eternity, is dramatically accented by the usual portrayals of Time as an old man with a scythe, and Death as a grinning skeleton with a scythe. We seek to avoid destruction by avoiding time.[21]

Time limitation in counseling, then, confronts the client in order to grapple with conflicting expectations. "The greater the ambiguity as to the duration of treatment, the greater the influence of child time on unconscious wishes and expectations. The greater the specificity of duration of treatment, the more rapidly and appropriately is child time confronted with reality and the work to be done."[22] For Mann the anxiety that is aroused in a time-limited contract of counseling is absolutely necessary. We might go so far as to say that the counselee's attempt to deny the passage of time is at the root of his or her relational problems in the first place.

In order to fulfill the second goal of pastoral counseling, the issue of time must be considered on a theological level. The meaning of time and timelessness has been of considerable importance to several theologians. Humanity is guilty and full of doubt, according to Tillich, but humanity is also anxious because of its creaturely finitude. Barth considers the temporality of human life an unsettling givenness. "A human self-understanding genuinely oriented by a general picture of man will be halted by the riddle of human temporality, and will have to be content to assert that we must live our life in the absolute uncertainty given with this riddle because we are not asked whether we would prefer a different possibility."[23] A sense of time is part of our existence, and it is within the sense of time that humans are dealt with by God in a covenantal relationship and in which the human counterpart of human relationality takes place. "A man without an awareness of history, without definite pictures of what was and the patience to learn from them, would be an escapist, running away from reality and God, and quite unreliable in his dealings with his fellow men."[24] To deny time and its passing is to embrace sin and irresponsibility. Yet, according to Barth, the temptation to denial and the attempt to rise above temporality is common to humankind.

H. Richard Niebuhr also emphasizes the place of time in understanding what it is to be human. In *The Responsible Self: An Essay in Christian Moral Philosophy* Niebuhr writes:

> The past and the future are not the no-longer and the not-yet: they are extensions of the present. They are the still-present and the already-present. . . . My interpersonal past also is with me in all my present meetings with other selves. It is there in all my love and guilt. The self does not leave its past behind as the moving hand of a clock does; its past is inscribed into it more deeply than the past of geologic formations is crystallized in their present form. As for the future, the not-yet, it is present in my now in expectations and anxieties, in anticipations and commitments, in hopes and fears. To be a self is to live toward the future and to do so not only in the form of purposiveness, but also of expectation, anticipation, anxiety, and hope. Past, present, and future are dimensions of the active self's time-fullness. They are always with it from the moment it has realized that "I am I."[25]

For Niebuhr, as for Barth and Tillich, time operates within the realm of relationships. Humans have memory in terms of relationships with important persons such as parents. In a similar fashion the future is understood in terms of relationships with others. Future relationships are understood through a memory of "images and patterns of interpretation, with attitudes of trust and suspicion, accumulated in its biographical and historical past. It comes to its meetings with the Thou's and It's with an a priori equipment that is the heritage of its personal and social past."[26] To this we could add Barth and his notion that all human relationships are made manifest by time. According to Barth, my fellow human being "does not confront me as an abstract idea, but for good or evil in his historical reality, in the totality of what he was and is and will be, and in this totality as the Thou without whom I could not be a human I."[27]

In my own work with John Patton, the place of time is central in marriage and family life. We argued that to be human is to care, and that caring takes place in the caring of the generations. No matter what one's family structure may be, that is, whether one is single and living alone or within a nuclear or blended family, one cares in terms of at least three generations: one's own, the one before, and the next.[28] All caring is bounded by time, and God has given us the responsibility of having dominion over creation through our generational caring.

From a pastoral theological perspective, time, or one's understanding of time, has been called a useful diagnostic tool by some theologians. Charles E. Brown has recently completed a study that investigated notions of time among disturbed psychiatric patients and their pastoral counselors. Brown found that there are several time typologies based on theological thinking and dynamic psychology:

> It is possible to formulate a helpful typology of temporal exaggerations which serve the various ego defenses. These distortions of the three temporal dimensions range from the most exaggerated elaboration of the infantile neurosis produced in the Oedipal conflict to the psychic numbing which results from the anticipatory dread of being overwhelmed by the future. Whatever

the temporal imbalance, however, *authentic existence is clearly eschatological existence,* i.e., existence character- ized by *acceptance of the past, openness in the present, and commitment to the future.* This eschatological existence, in turn, is wrought by the courageous confrontation and assimilation of one's own finitude, the possible meaninglessness of existence, and one's future "end- time." (Italics are Brown's)[29]

The limitation of time need not always be faced with dread by those who suffer. This point has been made clear by many liberation theologians. For many the end of the current time is the beginning of liberation and freedom from the bonds of oppression. Civil rights leaders intone this attitude in the exclamation "How long? Not long." The motivation of the realistic end of the present time can, therefore, offer hope that what is *now* does not have to be. Time-limited counseling takes this very powerful point made to us by theological anthropology and eschatology.[30]

Conclusion

Parish pastoral counseling has a peculiar context. While some critics believe that all persons in need should be referred, I have pointed to the legitimacy and necessity for parish pastoral counseling. Pastoral counseling in the parish has specific goals such as helping people help themselves while remaining part of the faith community, and providing the pastor with material rich in theological significance. These goals of pastoral counseling can be attained by the parish minister. The achievement of these goals is complicated by the significance of time in pastoral counseling—in a pragmatic and in a theological sense. Time is limited for everyone, and that is what it is to be human. Time-limited counseling places this reality in bold relief. In the following chapters, the pastor will learn how to engage the process of time-limited pastoral counseling.

Notes

1. Jackson W. Carroll, "The Professional Model of Ministry—Is It Worth Saving?" *Theological Education*, Spring 1985, pp. 7-48.

2. Alastair V. Campbell, *Professionalism and Pastoral Care* (Philadelphia: Fortress Press, 1985), p. 44.

3. Ibid., chapter 3 ("The Professional Captivity of Pastoral Care"), pp. 43ff.

4. For a discussion of the concepts of mind both in modern and pre-modern thought including that of several theologians see Charles Hampden-Turner, *Maps of the Mind* (New York: Collier Books, 1982).

5. See William A. Clebsch and Charles R. Jaekle, *Pastoral Care in Historical Perspective* (Englewood Cliffs, N.J.: Prentice-Hall, 1964), and John T. McNeill, *A History of the Cure of Souls* (New York: Harper & Bros., 1951).

6. E. Brooks Holifield, *A History of Pastoral Care in America* (Nashville: Abingdon Press, 1983).

7. Jonathan Edwards, *A Treatise Concerning Religious Affections*, 1746, ed. John E. Smith (New Haven: Yale University Press, 1959).

8. For two histories of this modern movement see Allison Stokes, *Ministry After Freud* (New York: Pilgrim Press, 1986), and Edward E. Thornton, *Professional Education for Ministry* (Nashville: Abingdon Press, 1970). Both of these histories point to some of the problems that arose in this new form of education and practice of pastoral care and counseling. Some of the problems pointed to by these two authors are similar to those pointed to by Carroll and Campbell, cited above. Both histories, however, point to the true struggle that most of the early leaders in the field had to maintain theological and ecclesiastical integrity while incorporating new educational and practical methods.

9. See Seward Hiltner, *Pastoral Counseling* (Nashville: Abingdon Press, 1981); Paul B. Maves, ed., *The Church and Mental Health* (New York: Charles Scribner's Sons, 1953); Russell L. Dicks, *Pastoral Work and Pastoral Counseling: An Introduction to Pastoral Care* (New York: Macmillan, 1951). Others began to see that there was a mutual fertilization between psychology and theology that needed to be exploited. See Don S. Browning, *Atonement and Psychotherapy*

(Philadelphia: Westminster Press, 1967) and David E. Roberts, *Psychotherapy and the Christian View of Man* (New York: Charles Scribner's Sons, 1950).

10. Seward Hiltner, *Preface to Pastoral Theology* (Nashville: Abingdon Press, 1958).

11. Ibid., pp. 219-22.

12. John Patton, *Is Human Forgiveness Possible?* (Nashville: Abingdon Press, 1985).

13. More about the development of dynamic personality theory is located in Salvatore R. Maddi, *Personality Theories*, rev. ed. (Homewood, Ill.: The Dorsey Press, 1972).

14. Hiltner, *Pastoral Counseling*, pp. 72-73.

15. Ibid., pp. 73-74

16. Ibid., pp. 75-76.

17. Ibid., p. 78.

18. Ibid.

19. James Mann, *Time-Limited Psychotherapy* (Cambridge, Mass.: Harvard University Press, 1973), p. 9.

20. Ibid., pp. 5-6.

21. Ibid., p. 7

22. Ibid., p. 11.

23. Karl Barth, *Church Dogmatics*, eds. G. W. Bromiley and T. F. Torrance, vol. 3, pt. 2, *The Doctrine of Creation*, trans. Bromiley et al. (Edinburg: T. & T. Clark, 1960), p. 514.

24. Ibid., p. 539.

25. H. Richard Niebuhr, *The Responsible Self: An Essay in Christian Moral Philosophy* (New York: Harper & Row, 1963), pp. 92-93.

26. Ibid., pp. 95-98.

27. Barth, *The Doctrine of Creation*, pp. 521ff.

28. John Patton and Brian H. Childs, *Christian Marriage and Family: Caring for Our Generations* (Nashville: Abingdon Press, 1988).

29. Charles E. Brown, *Time as a Determinant in Pastoral Processes: An Examination of the Conception of Time in the Works of Sigmund Freud and John Macquarrie and in Selected Cases of Pastoral Care with Implications for Pastoral Theology and Pastoral Counseling*, unpublished Ph.D. dissertation, Princeton Theological Seminary, 1982, pp. 446-47.

30. For a fuller account of the relationship of suffering and hope from a biblical theological perspective see J. Christiaan Beker, *Suffering and Hope* (Philadelphia: Fortress Press, 1987).

2

Defining Time-limited Counseling

Time-limited or short-term pastoral counseling has particular characteristics of which the pastor needs to be aware. In addition, time-limited counseling is best suited and is helpful to a certain kind of presenting problem brought by the counselee. It also is imperative to keep in mind that certain people are suited better for this type of counseling than are others. It is important to match the person in need—and their presenting problem—with the type of counseling described in this book.

Time-limited counseling is far more than just a counseling process with a prescribed beginning and ending time.[1] Time and its limitation has both a pragmatic and theological, anthropological significance. Time is important because there seems to be so little of it, and the limitation of our time tells us something about what it is to be human. We are caught in our desire to live in timelessness in the face of the reality of our finitude. At the same time we are hopeful of the end of our troubling time. When we are faced with this conflict our creatureliness is underscored and we are forced to confront our responsibilities. To paraphrase Barth, the one who has no concept of time is an escapist and irresponsible in his or her dealings with fellow humans. Some time-limited therapists, such as Mann, argue that the anxiety that is aroused with a prescribed ending of counseling is the touchstone of this kind of counseling.

Time-limited counseling therefore can offer the pastor a way of managing his or her counseling responsibilities while it underscores a basic theological principle. It also offers the pastor a way to deal with an essential issue facing all persons, no matter how they may define their problem. Time-limited counseling does, however, require a particular procedure that is best suited for a particular type of problem brought by a particular type of person.

Principles of Time-Limited Counseling

According to Bauer and Kobos there are seven basic principles unique to time-limited counseling.[2] I outline these principles with some additional clarifying material borrowed from other theorists.

Principle One. The counselor is active rather than passive in the counseling process. The counselor is not a passive interpreter of behavior but is an active participant in the counseling, sometimes confronting the counselee but at all times allowing for his or her own emotions to come into play in the process. According to some researchers in time-limited counseling, the counselor involved in brief counseling will have as much to say as the counselee. "It is striking to compare pages of written transcripts of long-term and brief therapy. While the former will show long productions by the patient interspersed with brief comments by the therapist, the brief therapy transcripts show almost equal productions by patient and therapist, both producing relatively brief material at each interchange."[3] In many ways this stance seems to fly in the face of what may have been learned in basic pastoral care courses in seminary. Indeed there is a major difference. In basic pastoral care many have learned to respond passively to whatever the parishioner may have to say, no matter where the material may lead. In time-limited counseling there is no time for free associations or regressions to whatever material comes to mind. The counseling is problem-centered and focused on a particular problem with limited time to come to a resolution.

Principle Two. The Focal Relational Problem (FRP) agreed upon by both the counselor and counselee is the exclusive material for each counseling session. Prior to the beginning of a course of time-limited counseling an evaluation session or two (chapter 3) is performed in which the counselor and the counselee have clearly described a circumscribed problem (FRP) and that is the focus for each counseling session. All discussion and each intervention will relate directly to that problem. This demands the active participation of the counselor to help the counselee keep the focus and solve the problem. Besides keeping the focus there is a secondary gain in the counselor's activity. As Bauer and Kobos have said, "Successful therapeutic work on a specific conflictual theme enhances self-esteem and has a positive impact on other aspects of the patient's functioning."[4] Another secondary gain is made when keeping the focus clear and the counselor active: the counselor communicates that the problem is manageable, and the counselor is truly interested in the problem and the counselee. This interest, coupled with the time limitation, assures the properly selected counselee (see pages 43-50) that optimism is justified for accomplishing the goal and it can be dealt with in a short period of time. "At the same time, the therapist indicates that it is up to the patient to do most of the work. The therapist frequently makes comments which highlight the patient's responsibilities and is quick to intervene when the patient tries to sit back and let the therapist do the work."[5] The counseling is truly an interactive process and not one of a passive expert listening to a struggling non-expert. Both have something at stake in the process, though ultimate responsibility rests with the counselee.

Principle Three. The counseling is a process of two allies dealing with a particular problem, and this alliance is established early in the relationship. From the first interview after the evaluation the counselor must communicate to the counselee that the counseling is a collaborative endeavor. In part this is communicated through the counselor's activity and focus on the FRP. In addition to this, the counselor concentrates on the counselee's positive side of his or her ambivalence. Rather than dealing exclusively with his or her weaknesses (flights into infantile timelessness), the counselor concentrates on the strengths and urges for growth including the decision to enter into counseling in the first place. My own image of this therapeutic alliance is of the counselor and the counselee rolling up their sleeves at the beginning of the counseling session with the exclamation "Now, let's get to it. Let's get to work!"

Principle Four. The counselor persistently points out resistance in the counselee to solving the FRP when it arises. One of the ironies of human behavior is that living with the uncomfortable because it is familiar at times seems preferable to living with the anxiety of facing or doing something new. At least, so it seems, the chronically uncomfortable is old hat and well known and therefore preferable to what appears to be the unknown and the unfamiliar. The counselor must be resolute in confronting the counselee whenever the counselee resists doing something to change, particularly as it relates to the FRP. "The therapist actively identifies and examines patient resistance and encourages the patient to practice more adaptive and collaborative behaviors."[6] The counselor's indication of resistance encourages the therapeutic alliance, forces the activity of the counselor around the FRP, and keeps hope alive by maintaining the impression that the problem can be solved.

Principle Five. The feelings that the counselee may have about the counselor and the counselor's own feelings about the counselee are important issues for the counseling process. When feelings arise, particularly as they relate to the FRP, they should be discussed. A major premise of short-term counseling is that the counselee's FRP will be enacted and reenacted in three realms.

- in the counselee's past;
- in the counselee's daily life as reported to the counselor in the counseling session;
- in the relationship with the counselor.[7]

The counselor must be attentive to signs of feelings the counselee may have about him or her. Such signs as silence, anxiety, and the changing of subject could well indicate feelings about the counselor. It is appropriate for the counselor to ask about these signs and wonder out loud if they have anything to do with feelings about him or her. Likewise feelings that the counselor may have about the counselee, particularly centering upon resistance to solving the problem, are appropriate to express. Any frustration that the counselor may have is probably similar to frustration felt by others who are part of the counselee's life. The important thing is to check these things out, not in an accusatory way but in the spirit of collaboration and curiosity. The counselor's curiosity is important in that curiosity takes the counselor out of the authority position and puts him or her more in a collaborative one.

Principle Six. The purpose of counseling is to solve the presenting FRP. In dealing with the counselee the counselor constantly reminds him or her that problem solving is the issue of all counseling sessions. The counselor acts as a role model with assurance that interpersonal conflict is understandable and manageable and need not be seen as hopeless.

Principle Seven. Adherence to the time limitation of the counseling must be maintained. Under no circumstances should the counselee be given the opportunity to suppose that the counseling will continue beyond the prescribed duration agreed upon after the evaluation. This is not to say that the relationship with the pastor will end, for it may not. Pastors have many realms of relationship with parishioners that are not counseling ones. It is possible for the counseling to end prior to the agreed upon termination. In this case the counselee should understand that the remaining number of sessions are "in the bank" and can be used for follow-up as needed. Nonetheless, the total agreed upon number of sessions is the absolute limit. If, under certain circumstances, the counselee is clearly in need of further counseling or therapy then referral is indicated. The referral, however, should not be made until the counselee has an opportunity to try out what he or she has learned first. Acute disturbances of any kind should be attended to with immediacy.

The Time Frame

Time-limited counseling has been defined as one or two sessions to even twenty or more. Some counselors leave the number of sessions open-ended with a general understanding that the counseling will not last as long as six to nine months. With our understanding of the meaning of time and the avoidance of limitation, such open-ended time-limited counseling is easily subverted. "The failure to give time, that horror in all human hearts, full recognition has effectively obstructed efforts to establish a sound methodology of any short-form psychotherapy."[8]

For the purposes of this work I have selected ten sessions as constituting the duration of time-limited counseling. There is no particular theoretical reason for selecting this number. Research has not shown that ten or fourteen or any other number is better or any more helpful. According to Mann the number selected is arbitrary. "Long experience in psychotherapy suggested that twelve sessions might be adequate for the therapist to accomplish some amount of work with the patient. More important, to study the meaning of time in short-form psychotherapy, some arbitrary choice had to be made so that one could begin."[9] After an evaluation interview or interviews, the contract for ten sessions of counseling centering upon the FRP is made. The counselor reminds the counselee at the beginning of each session which session it is. At the end the counselor reminds the counselee which session is next and the number of sessions left.

Counselee Selection

Proper counselee selection is probably the most important element for the success of time-limited counseling. This makes it essential that the evaluation process be done with considerable detail and accuracy. While this places considerable responsibility on the diagnostic skills of the counselor, there are several evaluational criteria that can help even the relatively inexperienced counselor feel comfortable in proceeding. Many of these criteria are second nature to most pastors, but it is important to make them conscious and intentional. Following the guidelines will also make referral easier if that should be needed.

Time-limited counseling is best suited for what Gustafson has called highly motivated and "relatively healthy patients."[10] According to Peter E. Sifneos a five-point selection criteria must be met for there to be reasonable hope for a successful outcome. They are as follows:

1. The ability of the patient to have a circumscribed chief complaint.
2. Evidence of a give and take, or "meaningful relationship" with another person during early childhood.
3. Capacity to relate flexibly to the evaluator during the interview and to experience and express feelings freely.
4. Psychological sophistication—above average intelligence and psychological mindedness.
5. Motivation for change and not for symptom relief.[11]

The first criterion reminds us that any counselee who is not able to focus upon one chief complaint will not be able to use the limited amount of time productively. The ability to prioritize a problem among many potential problems is an indication that the counselee can tolerate a degree of anxiety and ambiguity and has the motivation to deal with a particular troublesome issue.

The ability to circumscribe points further to the patient's capability to select a whole area of conflicting wishes rather than simply to choose a superficial symptom or interpersonal difficulty. Such a capacity, of course, demonstrates that the awareness of the underlying conflicts whose resolution will enable him to eliminate his symptoms once and for all is present and predominates at this point.[12]

The circumscribed problem is arrived upon in the give-and-take of the counselor and the counselee during the evaluation session or sessions.

A positive response to the second criterion is essential because it can eliminate from consideration potentially disturbing and complicated treatment issues. According to Sifneos, "The word 'meaningful' involves offering something as well as receiving something in return."[13] The outline of psychodynamic psychology by Hiltner in chapter 1 can serve to help one understand this important diagnostic element. The infant or young child is most passive and receives food and affection from caretakers. When this caretaking is halted even for a moment the child feels displeasure and responds with screams and tears. As the child grows and begins to explore its world and becomes independent, the need to receive becomes more complicated. The child needs to feel safe in the exploration while feeling assured that if a need arises it will be met. If this assurance is compromised then the exploration and individuation stops.

> If the threat of separation immediately brings to the child the need to take, then the newly discovered pleasures of exploration must quickly be abandoned or some other kind of compromise must be established. The possibility of giving something to the mother in return instead of taking all from her is discovered as a new way of keeping her close. Thus a novel way of dealing with this dilemma is found.[14]

Often the child will make a gift of a favorite toy. Even toilet training, which is a most dramatic example of the child's growing separation from the caretaker, is used as a gift. Many a parent of a two-year-old child has been given the gift of a well placed bowel movement with an enthusiastic announcement and even a refusal to flush the toilet until all in the household have seen! "Altruism is the result of the give-and-take interaction and is, in the most sophisticated way, the logical extension of the early mother-child transaction."[15]

As the child grows, he or she is faced with ever more complicated ways of staying close in a relationship, while also striving to gain independence. The need for pleasure must be balanced with the needs and desires of others in the relationship. The child who develops well and is lucky enough to be in a stable relationship with significant others soon learns that he or she may have to give up some pleasure in order to maintain the relationship. "Thus the individual who in his early life is prepared to make sacrifices for the sake of someone else, and who is willing to take risks and deny himself some pleasure, learns very quickly through this experience how to deal with people."[16]

In the evaluation stage, the counselor must be very attentive to the counselee's memories of relationships with significant caretakers in early life, from the age of five or six years and beyond. Clearly, highly inconsistent relationships with parents and siblings could mark trouble spots. The early death of a parent without other caretakers filling in the gaps, alcoholism in a parent, traumatic divorces with the shuffling around of children, and physical or sexual abuse in early childhood could compromise the development of an early meaningful relationship.

A significant early relationship with the development of what Sifneos calls *altruism* will more than likely help the counselee to positively fulfill the third criterion. The need to be defensive and suspicious of the counselor will be minimal. It must be understood that most people will be initially uneasy at the beginning of the evaluation interview. As the interview proceeds and if the counselor demonstrates his or her genuine interest in the counselee and the counselee's history, then this uneasiness should subside and a flowing give-and-take should develop. The counselor has a certain responsibility in allowing the counselee to fulfill this criterion. If the counselor is active, inter-active, direct, and positive in the history taking and the clarification, then the positive counselee should respond in kind. Defensiveness throughout the evaluation stage, most likely demonstrated with vague or minimal answers to questions, would exclude this counselee from consideration for time-limited counseling, and a referral should be considered.

While the fourth criterion seems to imply that advanced education is necessary, and though it may be helpful, it is not sufficient. More important than education is the issue of psychological mindedness.

> This term implies a familiarity with psychological constructs; it refers to an ability to deal with conflicting states, to tolerate paradoxical situations, and to exhibit behavioral patterns appropriate to such occurrences. For example, a patient who is convinced that a stomach pain which occurs whenever he has a fight with his supervisor at work must be due exclusively to physical factors, and who refuses to investigate the possibility that psychological issues may be associated with it, does not show evidence of psychological sophistication.[17]

I have often used a common, simple test in my own evaluation process that will get at the psychological mindedness of a potential counselee. In listening to a counselee talk about anger at work or at school I will ask: "Have you ever had the experience of being angry at somebody at work, say a boss, and then go home and kick the dog?" It is not so much that I receive a positive response to such a question. What is important is that the counselee understand the dynamic that I have described, that the question asks about displacement (though maybe not using such language), and that there be other analogous occurrences in the counselee's own life.

The final criterion is one of measuring motivation. Does the counselee want to change behavior more or less permanently, or is the desire only for palliative relief? In part this question asks the counselee for some level of responsibility in managing his or her own life. Simply put: is the counselee ready to get to problem solving and take an active role in problem solving, or is he or she wanting to be passive and receive what could only be an unrealistic fantasy of an omnipotent pastor granting relief?

Many pastors fail to adhere to this criterion in part because it can prick their own fantasies of omnipotence. It is tempting to buy into a counselee's dependence wherein he or she may say, "Oh pastor, only you can help me. I know you can." It is important to avoid these pleas and other more subtle ones. Pastoral counseling is helping people to help themselves. In time-limited counseling it is absolutely essential.

In addition to these five criteria, there should be added at least two others. Does the counselee have a certain curiosity about what makes him or her tick? In many ways this falls within the issue of psychological mindedness, but it is also in line with the issue of motivation. A certain excitement about getting to the bottom of a problem is the best measure of this curiosity. The second is the counselee's ability to make some sacrifice in the counseling process. This is best gauged in the counselee's willingness to come to appointments on time and regularly. Counselees do sometimes miss appointments, but anyone who misses them more than once without prior notification probably is not willing to make the existential sacrifice needed for problem-solving counseling to be successful.

Another way of measuring the willingness to sacrifice is the issue of charging fees for counseling. It has been my own experience that pastors can charge for their counseling time. In our culture most people expect to pay for the professional services they receive. In the church setting, a pledge is one sign of this. If the counselee is not a member of the church, a donation to the deacon's fund or the pastor's discretionary fund is appropriate. If fees are charged, possibly based on a sliding scale used by a local social service agency, it is best that the judicatory to whom the pastor is accountable be advised and informed.

In general, any potential counselee who cannot fulfill the five basic (and two contextual) criteria of time-limited counseling should be referred to other helping people. The pastor who cannot feel comfortable with the counselee's response to him or her should consider a consultation with another pastoral counselor or helping professional, or outright referral. The issue of consultation and referral will be discussed in detail later.

There are presenting problems that will arise in the evaluation that should immediately rule out further counseling. Significant or repeated suicide gestures or ideation warrant an immediate referral. Time-limited counseling is also not effective in dealing with chronic alcoholism or other substance abuse. Addiction is one of the most difficult problems that a person can face and often needs medical supervision as well as the long-term care of such groups as Alcoholics Anonymous. In addition persons who have had chronic psychiatric problems, including psychiatric hospitalizations, should be referred. There are other types of situations which are not suitable for time-limited counseling, and they will be discussed in the next chapter. Of course, referral does not mean the end of pastoral care, but only of formal pastoral counseling. Support, religious counsel, and the sacraments are forms of pastoral care that any pastor is called to perform no matter who else, if anyone, is involved in other forms of care.

Generally the types of problems best suited for time-limited and problem-solving pastoral counseling are those problems that healthy people constantly face. But they get stuck. Minor depressions, problems at work or with work relationships, some forms of minor obsessionalism, and common grief are usually amenable to this approach to counseling. Of course, the treatment criteria must always be met.

The Attitude of the Pastor

Time-limited counseling demands a great deal of pre-assessment by both the counselee and the counselor. Of greatest importance, the pastor cannot be passive and uninvolved in the process. In time-limited pastoral counseling, the pastor and counselee are not in a subject-object relationship but should be closer to what Buber has called an I-Thou relationship. To quote Tillich:

> The basic principle for the attitude of pastoral counseling is mutuality. The counselor must participate in the situation of the person needing care. This participation expresses itself not only in words of acceptance, but also in ways of communicating to the counselee the fact

that the counselor was and is in the same situation. This can be done by telling a concrete story in which the counselor experienced the same negativities for which the counselee needs care. It can be in words which make it clear to the counselee that the counselor understands well on the basis of his own experience.[18]

The motivation for change; the curiosity of what it is to be human; the ability to clearly state what the situation is; the basic ability to be altruistic in spite of conflicts with our own desires; and the limitation of our time are realities for both the pastor and his or her counselee. Time-limited pastoral counseling, in part because of its selection process, in part because of its counseling structure, and in part because of its time boundedness, facilitates this mutuality.

This form of counseling does exclude, with the generally trained pastor, many of God's creatures in need of mutuality and healing. These people are not excluded from this experience totally, but they do need to be referred to those other helpers, including secular healers, who are specially trained and have access to resources that can be helpful when entering into a relationship with those in need. Remember that many of these people will come to the pastor first, and through the relationship with the pastor, will find help that is needed. Indeed they may find help because they first went to the caring pastor who, though he or she might not have been able to participate in the counseling right away, was caring enough and knowledgeable enough about his or her own limitations to refer them to a specialized practitioner.

Conclusion

In time-limited counseling, the activity of the counselor in collaboration with the counselee in solving a Focal Relational Problem is a basic signature. There is a mutuality and a give-and-take in the process and it transpires during a prescribed and definite period of time.

Any person not able to fulfill the basic criteria for time-limited counseling should be considered for referral.

In the next chapter I will outline the process of evaluation keeping in mind the elements of time-limited counseling and for whom this type of specialized ministry is best suited.

Notes

1. In addition to the sources cited in this chapter outlining the definition and selection criteria for time-limited counseling, consider Robert J. Ursano and Robert E. Hales, "A Review of Brief Individual Psychotherapies" *American Journal of Psychiatry*, 1986, 143:1507-17, a helpful overview of the time-limited process.

2. Gregory P. Bauer and Joseph C. Kobos, *Brief Therapy: Short-Term Psychodynamic Intervention* (Northvale, N.J.: Jason Aronson, 1987), pp. 6-9.

3. Walter V. Flegenheimer, *Techniques of Brief Psychotherapy* (New York: Jason Aronson, 1982), p. 7.

4. Bauer and Kobos, *Brief Therapy*, p. 6.

5. Flegenheimer, *Techniques of Brief Psychotherapy*, p. 8.

6. Bauer and Kobos, *Brief Therapy*, p. 7.

7. Lester Luborsky, *Principles of Psychoanalytic Psychotherapy, A Manual for Supportive-Expressive Treatment* (New York: Basic Books, 1984), pp. 110ff.

8. James Mann, *Time-Limited Psychotherapy* (Cambridge, Mass.: Harvard University Press, 1973), p. 12.

9. Ibid., p. 15.

10. James Paul Gustafson, *The Complex Secret of Brief Psychotherapy* (New York: W. W. Norton, 1986), p. 286.

11. Peter E. Sifneos, *Short-Term Dynamic Psychotherapy*, 2nd ed. (New York: Plenum Medical Book Company, 1987), p. 27.

12. Ibid., p. 28.

13. Ibid., p. 31.

14. Ibid.

15. Ibid., p. 32.

16. Ibid.

17. Ibid., p. 39.
18. Paul Tillich, "The Theology of Pastoral Care," *Clinical Education for the Pastoral Ministry,* proceedings of the Fifth National Conference on Clinical Pastoral Education, Advisory Committee on Clinical Pastoral Education, 1958.

3

Pastoral Evaluation and Diagnosis

While greeting parishioners at the church door after worship one Sunday, the pastor, Beth, noticed Edgar lingering just inside the sanctuary. The pastor had known Edgar for the entire three years that she had been minister of the small congregation in rural central Pennsylvania. She did not know him terribly well, for though he was a member of the congregation, along with his wife and family, he worshiped somewhat irregularly and participated only in a limited way in other church functions. They did have a cordial relationship, however. The pastor sensed that Edgar had something to say to her, and he was waiting for the last person to leave before he would speak. The following conversation took place.

Pastor: Well, good morning, Edgar. Nice to see you today.

Edgar: Good morning, Beth. You have a wonderful way of preaching. I know I don't come to hear you near enough.

Pastor: Thank you, Edgar. I do like to see you worship with us. (Silence for a few uncomfortable seconds) Is there something I can do for you?

Edgar:	Well, no . . . I don't know. I guess you are going home now for dinner with your family.
Pastor:	Well, yes I am. John and the kids have gone ahead. I have to lock up. Why don't you come with me while I do that, and we can chat for a few moments.
Edgar:	Sure, but I don't want to take too much of your time. (They walk together and lock the back door.) I don't know really what I want, but I thought last night that I'd come to church today and see if I could talk to you. I know I am not the most active member of the church, but I do honor my pledge. It's not much.
Pastor:	We appreciate your pledge and do want you to feel comfortable here. I sense, though, that is not what you want to talk about.
Edgar:	Right, but you have to go and I am not really sure what it is I want to say. I just know that I wanted to contact you. Maybe some other time would be better.
Pastor:	Fine. I'd like very much to see you. How about tomorrow after work? I'll be in my office . . . say four-thirty.
Edgar:	Thank you, Beth. I'll be there.

Edgar had something he needed to talk about. While he may not have had a very clear idea of what was troubling him, it was clear to the pastor that he had something to say. In this case there was little time to have much of a conversation, and at any rate Edgar was not ready. It seemed that he just wanted to know if the pastor was available. She showed herself to be available and made an appointment to see Edgar in an atmosphere where he would have the time to say whatever he had to say.

At this point Beth had no idea of what was on Edgar's mind. He could be considering dropping his church membership or he could be having some difficulty at home or work. Beth made the appointment to offer Edgar the opportunity to express himself to her. Her job would be to listen to him, evaluate what he had to say, and offer him advice about the matter. At this point Beth had no idea that counseling necessarily was one option of help she could offer. Coming to that conclusion would depend not only upon Edgar's needs but also upon how she structured the appointment interview and made her evaluation. At any rate, it was to be a joint endeavor. How Beth structured the interview was important to achieve the goal of assessment, but Edgar also needs to ask for help if in fact he requires it.

Diagnosis is probably the most important aspect of any kind of counseling. Without some preliminary form of diagnosis and evaluation, any ensuing pastoral conversation will become meandering and pointless dialogue, at best. At worst, it will become an empty monologue carried out by the pastor, possibly full of exhortation and wisdom, but having no real value to the counselee. Diagnosis is a disciplined form of engaging the counselee and listening to the responses. It is directed conversation. The very best diagnosticians that I have ever known are those people who know how to listen. It is not just listening, however, that makes them good diagnosticians. The listening process must be organized and structured so that the pastor and the counselee both know what to listen for.

The noun *diagnosis* is derived from the Greek *dia*, meaning through or thoroughly, and the noun *gnōsis*, meaning knowledge. The term implies a dynamic process of knowing and a revision of that knowing. To know, through conversation, is a process and never a single event frozen in some static point in time. Diagnosing a situation entails learning not only what is presented, but also its history and its likely future course. Perhaps it was Herbert Spencer who said that perception is essentially diagnosis. This underscores the dynamic quality of diagnosis as a perception of incoming data and stimulation with the rational evaluation of what that data means.

The diagnosis, or learning, will alter when the object of perception is seen in different angles, contexts, lighting, and under varying forms of stress or anxiety. For this reason, a diagnosis is always tentative and not something chiseled in stone. To understand a psychological diagnosis as static is to risk placing the person within the field of physical objects with no will, self-direction, or self-consciousness. The context of our diagnosis has much to do with what kind of diagnosis is made in the first place. The following is an example of how context can influence a diagnosis. I see a child being spanked by a man. I would be alarmed if the man is not the child's father. If I were to learn that the man was the child's uncle with parental authority, my reaction would change, no doubt, no matter how I felt about corporal punishment. Time and place and context can alter our perceptions. Diagnosis of counselees will also alter over time in other places, and in differing contexts. In counseling, the diagnosis should change especially if the counseling is helpful.

The Counseling Office

The pastor's office is part of the context when making a pastoral diagnosis. The pastor's office must be as soundproof as possible. Nothing is more inhibiting to the counselee than to be able to hear even slightly discernible conversations behind closed doors either while waiting to go into the pastor's study or while in the study. If the pastor's study is not soundproofed, you may consider using "white sound" machines.

These simple electric boxes emit an inoffensive sound which imitates a fan. They do help to mute the sounds of conversation outside the walls.

The counseling office will likely be the pastor's own study at the church. The study is a room that will reflect the personality of the pastor. There may be diplomas on the wall, various works of art, especially religious art, books, personal awards, and possibly family photographs. Whatever the decor, the office should be comfortable. While reflecting the taste of the primary occupant, these objects must not be allowed to distract either the pastor or the counselee. Of course any comment made about the decor of the office is material for formulating a diagnosis. Is there any particular interest in any religious theme depicted by artwork? What kinds of comments does the counselee make about family photographs? Do such comments tell the pastor something about the counselee's own family?

In addition to soundproofing, obtain comfortable chairs for both the pastor and counselee. Never should the pastor sit behind a desk during a counseling session. The pastor should sit across, slightly at an angle, from the counselee. Comfortable chairs are important. The pastor may have a slightly more comfortable chair—after all he or she uses it more each day and should be allowed that luxury. Proper lighting is also important. The pastor may want some side tables for coffee or a note pad. There should also be a prominent place for facial tissues.

The Diagnostic Process

Edgar arrived for his appointment with the pastor a few minutes early. He waited for her in her secretary's empty office. There was a pot of coffee ready. He, taking advantage of a sign over the pot offering the beverage to all who wanted, was sipping his cup of coffee slowly. Beth opened her door and invited him into her office. He took his seat across from Beth's overstuffed wing chair, and the interview began. Here follows the structural process of Beth's evaluational or diagnostic interview. Each step of the process will be described and how much time it should take within the evaluation process. It is assumed that this first interview will last about sixty minutes.

During the evaluation process Beth took notes on a legal pad. She not only took notes pertaining to information, but she also made notes to herself concerning impressions she had about Edgar: his mood, his comfort or discomfort, and any other thing that "just seemed important."

Joining

The first task of the pastoral counselor in the diagnostic or evaluational interview, and to a lesser extent at the beginning of each interview, is to put the counselee at ease. In part this has something to do with empathy as an attitude of being with the person and being interested in his or her present situation. One of the best ways of doing this is a process family therapists call "joining." Joining makes explicit the implicit similarities of experience between the counselor and the counselee. A very senior colleague of mine is fond of saying that there virtually is not a single person who has entered his office with whom he does not have something in common. As we increase in age and experience this is true of any of us, and it is certainly true of my very experienced colleague. There is usually something that we may have in common with most people who enter our offices if only the same neighborhood, geographical origin, ethnicity, education, or interests. Joining is not just small talk before the important talk begins. It lets the counselees know that you are interested in them as whole persons and not just with their problems; that you have some notion of where they have been and who they are because you have shared similar experiences. Joining does not need to take long—five or so minutes at most.

Pastor: What kind of work do you do, Mr. S.?
Mr. S.:   I'm a farmer, mostly soybeans and potatoes.
Pastor: I'm a city boy myself, but I sure do remember my summers on my cousin's farm in Missouri.
Mr. S.:   Missouri! I have family in Hannibal.
Pastor: My father was raised there . . .

The above brief conversation from my own clinical practice illustrates what could be considered a mundane example of conversation which helped to create a bond of cooperation. Making too much of this connection could divert the pastor from dealing with the issues at hand, to be sure; but it is my experience, particularly with inexperienced counselors, that this important beginning stage is sacrificed by a desire to ask too many impersonal questions.

During the "joining time" the pastor can take notes of some very important information. Is the counselee anxious? How is this anxiety shown? How is the counselee dressed—well groomed or not? Does the counselee have any speech characteristics or other physical qualities that should be noted? Is there eye contact? How was the opening handshake? All of this information will be used to make the diagnostic impression, and it should be noted.

The importance of joining cannot ever be underestimated. It, along with a comfortable and secure working place, is an invaluable part of initiating a pastoral contact and encouraging confidence in the counseling process. Through joining, the counselee is told that he or she is a valuable human being worthy of respect, no matter what the supposed problem may be. Joining also lets the counselee know that the pastor values him or her as a human with interests and a life that may not involve the "symptoms" at all. If the counselee feels that the counselor is interested only in his or her pathology, then the counselee may feel that the counselor is a rather one-dimensional person at best or one with prurient voyeuristic interest at the worst. Joining, in our one-hour sequence, will take five minutes.

The Presenting Problem

The counselee begins at this point to describe the problem. The way in which the problem is presented is the best diagnostic tool that the pastor has. More often than not, those who are involved in counseling, especially those who are relative beginners, forget this vital and primary source for formulating a working diagnosis. The simple question "What brings you to speak to me at this time?" should be the very first question asked after the joining is accomplished. While the counselee may respond with rather vague answers to this question, the follow-up of clarifying questions by the pastor can sharpen and make more explicit the needs and desires that bring the counselee to the office. The task of clarification is best made through more or less indirect interview methods.

Pastor: What brings you to see me today?
Edgar: Well, I . . . I haven't been feeling well. Sort of out of it, I guess.
Pastor: You have not been feeling on top of things lately?
Edgar: No, I just don't seem to have the zip I used to have.

Pastor: You have been kind of sluggish. How long has this been the case?

Edgar: Well, I don't really know. It has kinda been building. I suppose that it was just after my youngest married.

From this brief segment of Beth's interview, one can begin expressing, by using reflective language, the counselee's own feelings, and a diagnostic picture can be developed. In this case Beth's first impression was that Edgar's depression came to a head when his last child left home. Other matters that need to be questioned are who and where other family members are; if they are out of the home; under what circumstances did they leave home; the nature of the relationships; how things are going at work, and the like. The point is that listening, directly listening, to the counselee and how he or she expresses the problem is the most important source of diagnostic information.

What cannot be emphasized enough is that the presenting problem is a problem that the counselee owns by using his or her own language. The counselee describes the problem from a subjective point of view. The pastor then in turn uses this personal evaluation to open a dialogue that allows the material to become more objective and therefore manageable. The pastor should be attentive not only to what the feelings are but also to when they began, who else is involved, and where the problem becomes most critical—at work, at home, on vacation, or in other recreational contexts. It has been my own experience that most people come to the pastor when the problem is particularly acute, that is, at a head. For this reason most people have a fairly good idea of what it is that bothers them and have a fairly good knowledge of the history of the problem.

It is quite important that the pastor keep track of the time during this part of the initial interview. It is easy to let too much time go by with an interest on but one aspect of the presenting problem. Behavior such as excessive complaining or emotional displays (crying or anger) and the like can delay discussion of the issue that needs to be managed. In fact, an excessive amount of time expressing emotion or complaining may be typical of the counselee's unsuccessful approach to the problem. This kind of behavior can be a way of avoiding problem solving, or it can illustrate the hopelessness that the counselee may have toward an ability to deal with the problem. Of course if the counselee seems more content in discussing the problem than in actually trying to solve the problem, this in itself is a valuable piece of diagnostic information. The presenting part of the evaluation should take about fifteen minutes.

History Taking

In history taking the pastor learns important things about the counselee, including family history, educational background, work history, and medical history. It is important to know where the client grew up and with whom: who else was in the family (either kin or non-kin) and what were the relationships. Also important are such things as the frequency of moves from one house or state to another, and any memories about growing up. Try to ask in a summary way, when inquiring about family and place, about particular happy or sad memories that the counselee had in growing up. It is here also that the pastor can ask about the counselee's church background. If the counselee is married (or re-married) attempt to find out the duration of the marriage, how the spouse was met, and where they have lived during the marriage.

A brief educational and work history is also useful, particularly if the counselee has had a difficult time with schooling or has had difficulty in keeping a job for any significant period of time. If there has been a protracted schooling experience or various jobs in a short period of time, ask if any other person besides the counselee has been affected.

A particular medical history is also informative. Have there been any illnesses outside normal childhood illnesses? Have there been any accidents that required hospitalization? Has any family member needed prolonged medical attention? If so, when? It is also important to know if the counselee is currently seeing a medical practitioner and is being prescribed any medication. If the client does complain of even vague physical problems and does not have a medical practitioner, it is incumbent on the pastor to encourage that one be found for a physical. This attention to physical health cannot be overemphasized.

I always inquire of each potential counselee if there is any use of alcohol or other substances. If there is use of alcohol ask how much is used and if the counselee has ever wondered if too much is used. By asking these questions in a matter-of-fact, nonjudgmental way at least the counselee will know that you take such issues seriously and that the discussion of substance use is appropriate, even if the counselee does not tell you directly if there is a problem.

In a similar fashion, discuss the counselee's eating and sleeping habits. Make note if there is any disturbance of habitual eating and sleeping patterns that could indicate potential problems of either a physical nature, and therefore within the purview of a physician, or of a psychological nature, such as depression.[1] This history taking should occur in about fifteen minutes.

Previous Help

One aspect of the initial interview, which often is overlooked by many pastors, is the question of previous ways that the counselee has attempted to deal with the problem. This aspect of the interview is best begun with the simple question: What have you done in the past to attempt to solve this problem? This question is helpful for at least two reasons.

First, it will provide the pastor some basic information about what has been attempted in the past and what has worked and what hasn't. It is also important, no matter if what was attempted has or has not worked, to know the context of the attempt. The answer to this question will give the pastor a sharper vision of what may be done in the process of the counseling by exploiting what has worked in the past or by avoiding unsuccessful moves altogether.

Second, this question will also give the pastor some idea of the nature of the problem by understanding how resistant it is to change. In other words the failures of the past give the pastor some ideas to avoid, ideas to pursue, and a clearer idea of the nature and tenacity of the problem. If there have been other professionals involved, they may be contacted, with the written permission of the counselee. It would also be helpful to ask why they were not consulted again. The answer to this question could be quite telling. At this point the pastor could ask what the goals of counseling may be from the counselee's point of view. This question not only gives the pastor some notion of the problem, but it also influences whether the pastor is willing or able to be involved in the problem-solving process. Queries about previous help should take no longer than ten minutes.

Religious or Theological Issues

It is ironic and possibly even diagnostic itself that many pastors forget or deny a powerful evaluative tool ready at their disposal when they don their counseling cloaks. Often ignored is the very powerful language of our religious and theological tradition. The reasons for this neglect are many and varied, and many pastoral theologians and historical theologians have attempted to explain this phenomenon.[2] It has been my own experience that many pastors avoid using religious language in their counseling because it does not sound therapeutic enough or because it smacks of formulaic, simple, and self-satisfied pietism. In their attempt to loose themselves from the rational and rather dogmatic use of religious language in a pro- or prescriptive sense, many in the pastoral counseling movement have borrowed, at times willy nilly, the language of psychology. As our culture becomes more and more pluralistic and increasingly secular, religious language appears to many to have lost its clout. Like it or not, our culture has become sufficiently "psychologized" that it appears that the language of Freud dominates six days of the week and the language of the religious tradition owns Sunday at 11:00 in the morning, at best.

I am not at all sure that the people who come to counseling with a pastor are shy about talking about themselves in terms of religious language and the language of their religious tradition. While there may be a certain timidity in using such language and at times it is true that religious language can be a smokescreen blocking the issues at hand, most persons will follow the lead of the pastor in expressing themselves theologically. Not only that, such language has considerable power. Religious language is too often misunderstood as being exclusively apodictic, full of certainty, and there only for direction and order.

Ironically it was a psychiatrist, Edgar Draper, who in 1965 presented a brilliant study of how powerful is religious language in understanding people and their problems.[3] Draper and his colleagues were able to demonstrate that psychiatrists who were presented with transcript materials containing only the religious language of patients made remarkably similar diagnoses as did a panel of other psychiatrists who had access to more traditional psychiatric interview transcripts. Draper did not claim that religious language was in fact "sick," but that troubled people tended to use their religious language in such a way that it was somehow correlated to the way they understood themselves in other types of language. In addition it was concluded that certain people had an easier time talking about their problems in religious terms rather than in the often intimidating language of psychology. Religious language has the power to expose our deepest yearnings and conflicts.

Since the Draper study several non-psychiatrists have discussed the power of religious language in understanding our own and others' troubles. In *The Minister as Diagnostician*[4] Paul Pruyser argues that ministers and other religious workers should use religious and theological language in their counseling work. The counselee may ask questions about personal understanding of grace, God's providence, and what God expects of us. The questions are not just catechetical but are also questions that tell us how we think about ourselves and others. Most recently Wayne E. Oates, the well known pastoral theologian, has presented a similar work, *Behind the Masks: Personality Disorders in Religious Behavior,*[5] that, much like the Draper study, illustrates a correlation between psychiatric disorders and their religious manifestation.

A pastor can appreciate the power of a person's religion in his or her life, but the pastor should not subsume religious language within psychological systems of language any more than should the pastor subsume psychological language within a theological

system. Both language systems are ways of understanding and explaining the self and the self within the
world, though with critical differences. The language of
psychology (and psychiatry), while appearing value
free and objectively scientific, is in fact laden with
ethical valuation, as Don Browning has shown.[6] On the
other hand, religious language is laden with normative
notions, at times very explicit. Therefore, correlating
the two in any neat way is doomed to failure. While
both language systems attempt to tell us about
ourselves, they do it from very different perspectives.
The reduction of one language system into another is to
be avoided. Dialogue and even transformation of
preconceived notions in either direction, however, is
desirable.

While the pastor may wish to give a special place in
the evaluation or diagnostic interview for the exploration of religion and religious language, the topic is not
mandatory. The counselee's religious attitude can be
discussed in any of the stages of the diagnostic
interview. Certainly if the person's religious life is not
discussed in the other stages it would be appropriate for
it to be brought up at the end of the interview. The total
amount of time given to this could be ten to fifteen
minutes.

Concluding the Interview

If the pastor follows the above schedule for a
diagnostic interview and has been able to keep to the
time allotted, fifty or fifty-five minutes have passed. At
this time the pastor reviews with the counselee what
has transpired. The entire interview need not be
reviewed. At this stage the pastor attempts a recapitula-
tion of the counselee's presenting problem in words
close to those used by the counselee, then with some
rewording of the problem in the pastor's words. By

concluding the interview in this way, the pastor is signaling the counselee that the diagnosis is the result of a dialogical process that is ever open to revision and possibly even new construction. In addition the pastor can review the presenting problem in light of the information gained in the history taking, the counselee's previous attempts to solve the problem, and what the counselee hopes to achieve in working for new solutions. Critical at this point is an agreement between the pastor and the counselee on a clear identity or description for the focal relational problem (FRP).

At this time the pastor is not compelled to offer counseling to the counselee. In point of fact, the pastor may not be in a position to help the person. The pastor can, however, assure the counselee that there will be some help coming, either in a counseling agreement with the pastor or through a referral to another helping person.

A Sample Diagnostic Transcript

In the case of Edgar and his pastor, Beth, the following was learned in the diagnostic interview. After a very few minutes of joining (both of them are die-hard Penn State fans and the team had lost a game the previous Saturday), Edgar described his problem as being "out of sorts" and "kinda sluggish." It was also learned that the youngest child had just left home by marrying several months ago. It was also learned that Edgar was lethargic at work and was not having as much fun with one of his passions: a couples bowling league that he and his wife had helped to found. His wife had expressed some concern about him and had been supportive, but had also expressed some exasperation with his "moping" around the house on weekends.

Edgar was the youngest son of a career Army sergeant and a sometime schoolteacher. His two older sisters (one ten years older and the other seven years older) were both married and lived in the Midwest. They got together every other year or so and kept in contact by phone. Edgar had mixed feelings about his growing up. Because of his father's career, Edgar had lived in several exotic places including Germany and Spain and several interesting places in the United States. While Edgar considered this a real plus in his growing up, he also found the rather frequent moves difficult. As he said to Beth: "Just when I had developed friendships and when I was in high school with my first girlfriend it was time to move away. It seemed like every time I turned around it was time to say good-bye." His father went overseas alone on two occasions. Once was during the Korean War and the second time was to a hardship post (no family allowed) in Greenland. The first overseas duty was when Edgar was about seven and the other when he was thirteen. Edgar's mother was a homemaker for most of his growing up, though when he turned twelve she went back to work as an elementary schoolteacher. At the same time his next oldest sister went off to college. His oldest sister had already gone to college and married.

Edgar described his relationships with his parents as being very good, though he was closer to his mother than his father. "Dad worked very hard . . . and of course the Army would send him off every now and then. He was a gentle man and very smart. He was an aviation electronics technician and then later was a top sergeant administrator of other technicians. He had more medals on his chest than most officers. Sometimes civilians thought he was a general, he had so many medals. I thought it was great, but he always was very businesslike and would tell them that, no, he was just a sergeant and that he worked for generals. That kind of made me mad sometimes, because I was proud." His father died in 1980 of a stroke at the age of seventy-five. Edgar's father and mother were living with Edgar and his wife, Madge, when his father died. Two years after his father's death, his mother died of a heart attack.

Edgar met Madge when he was an electronics student at Penn State. Though he was very good at electronics, college was not for him, so after two years he dropped out of school and went to work with the local power company. After starting out servicing large transformers, he was now in a middle-management position supervising a district of seven maintenance crews. He likes his work most of the time. He does not get enough hands-on work, though he does try to get out into the field every chance he gets. Madge finished college (they dated two years and they were married when she was a senior nursing student and he was with the power company) and currently works in a pediatrics office as head nurse and administrator. He described his marriage as very good with the normal ups and downs. Most fighting was over child rearing or sometimes money.

Edgar and Madge have two children, both daughters. The eldest went to Penn State and married a classmate just a few months after Edgar's father's death. She and her husband have two children. The most recent grandchild was born two months ago. The daughter and her family live in California, and though Madge flew out just after the birth, Edgar could not go due to work responsibilities. They are planning a vacation in California this summer. Their second daughter married three months ago. Beth performed the ceremony. This daughter and her husband, both Penn State graduates, too, live in Ohio, where he is a law student and she is a paralegal in a private law firm. Edgar describes his relationship with his daughters as one of a doting father. Madge was the disciplinarian and he was admittedly the cream-puff. "They could get away with murder with me. I guess the biggest fight we ever got in was when Cindy (the eldest) turned sixteen and I surprised everyone by going out and buying her a used Volkswagen convertible. Lord, was Madge mad and was Sue (the youngest) envious. Madge said we could not afford the car, the insurance, and the maintenance, though I did most of that. She also yelled at me, 'You know you are going to have to get Sue one, too, in a couple of years, Diamond Jim!' Well, she was right, of course, and I did. Madge still calls me that sometimes. Diamond Jim, I mean." Edgar seemed to get some pleasure in telling Beth this story, for he had a wry smile on his face as he related it.

Edgar is in good health. He has some blood pressure problems but takes medication and sees his doctor twice a year. He has noticed that he wants to sleep more than usual but always wakes up in the morning still tired. Though he still has a healthy appetite, he says that he does not enjoy food as much lately.

When asked who else was involved in his "feeling out of sorts" he said that, of course, Madge was concerned. He said he also had a close friend at work who had noticed his lethargy. Edgar had snapped at his friend and some of the men he worked with. That was out of character for him, he said. He was concerned with this because now that his daughters were out of the house he wanted to be at his best for Madge. When they retired from their work they wanted to travel in Europe and to visit the children and their families. He wants to enjoy traveling and is worried that he would be an "old stick in the mud."

While growing up, Edgar and his family were not

very religious, he said. They only belonged to one church that he could remember—a Methodist church. When they went to church, it was usually an Army base chapel whose chaplains were always changing. When Cindy first came along, Edgar and Madge had joined the church that Beth now served. While never very active, they did worship more often than not, had pledged every year, and the daughters participated in youth fellowship. Edgar had respected the pastor who had preceded Beth and was sorry that he retired and moved away after serving the church for nearly twenty years. Beth sensed that Edgar respected her, too, and enjoyed their Penn State connection.

Edgar said he believed that God had called us to do our best and that was important. He did not have a sense of a personal God, though he thought that God was always around, even in the face of pain and tragedy. He found the church to be a comforting presence and was glad that he had worshiped at the same one for so long, in fact, nearly as long as he had worked for the power company. In contrast to his moving around so much as a kid, his job and the church gave him a sense of stability that he cherished. He did have some cynical feelings about certain religious figures and thought that most of them were interested in their own wealth and power. He also got frustrated with what appeared to him to be the overly political activity of his own denomination, but he thought that things usually work out in a way that in our own time we can't see or predict.

Edgar had never consulted a professional about his feelings. This was so mainly because the feelings were never so severe that he had been worried before, though they were at the same time not unfamiliar. The closest he had come to talking about his feelings was with the previous pastor after his father and mother died. His talks with the pastor both in the pastor's office and over coffee in a local diner before work were very helpful and important to him.

The conversation between Beth and Edgar ended with the following conversation.

Pastor: Edgar, we have to stop now, but first I want to go over a few things. Is that O.K.?

Edgar: (With a grin) Sure . . . what's the verdict doc?

Pastor: Well, as you say, you are out of sorts . . . not feeling just right. It seems that it sort of gets in the way of things at work with your friend and the people who work for you. You also tell me that Madge is a bit worried, too. Is that right?

Edgar: Yes, so far so good. You have been listening, for sure.

Pastor: Great. It seems that you have quite a bit to look forward to. I mean the grandchildren and maybe more coming soon. You and Madge have some plans in store, vacations, bowling league, and the like. I hear you say that you don't want to go into those things feeling sluggish. It also occurs to me that what you have been telling me is that while you have quite a bit to say "hello" to, you have also spent quite a bit of time saying "good-bye." You moved around quite a bit growing up, and when you finally settled down to work, raising a family, and the church here, you started saying good-bye all over again. Your parents died; Frank, who was here at the church for so long, moved to Florida; and the kids have left home. Lots of good-byes in your life.

Edgar: Yes, Beth. I guess I never thought of it like that before. I thought those days were over, but I guess they never are. People grow up and grow old. That doesn't mean that we have to like all the good-byes, does it?

Pastor: No, it doesn't. But at the same time, it is unavoidable. And besides, there are a lot of

75

hellos to say and live for, too. Isn't that what you want to do?

Edgar: (Thoughtfully) Yes.

Pastor: If you were to talk more to me or someone else about this, what would you hope to accomplish?

Edgar: Well, I don't really know. I sure want to feel like I have more vinegar, that is for sure. I guess I also want to stop looking back and spend a little more time looking forward . . . you know?

Pastor: I think that I do. Here is what I want to do, Edgar. How about if you and I get together next Monday at the same time? When we get together, why don't we see how things are going and see what else we could do to help you with this problem? Now it may be that you could benefit from talking to me some more, or maybe we could think of your seeing someone else, say Jim Philips over at the pastoral counseling center in the Methodist church. But before we talk about that, let's think about it for a week and put our heads together again next week. How does that sound?

Edgar: Sounds O.K. to me, though I sure think that talking to you helps. I feel better now getting some of this off my chest, but I think more talk will make some sense. I'll see you next week. I'll also make it to church more often.

Pastor: That would be fine, Edgar. I always like seeing you and Madge out there. At any rate, see you next Monday at 4:30.

Edgar: Thank you.

Conclusion

Diagnosis is not a label imposed by a professional upon a passive supplicant, rather it is a statement of a process that is gathered in the conversation between a helper and a person seeking help. For our purposes the diagnosis is also called the Focal Relational Problem

(FRP), and it is a statement of a problem first offered by the counselee and refined and clarified through the conversation with the pastor. The FRP is further clarified through the guided exploration of the counselee's life and environment by way of placing the FRP within the context of the counselee's growing up and maturational development. A counselee's religious life can make a powerful contribution to understanding the FRP throughout the evaluation.

In the next chapter, the process of the pastor's solidifying the diagnosis or FRP will be discussed. The pastor will learn how it is used to offer a course of short-term counseling for the counselee. In addition the issue of consultation and referral will also be discussed.

Notes

1. For a more detailed discussion of depression and depression's effects on the daily life of people see Roy W. Fairchild, *Finding Hope Again: A Guide to Counseling the Depressed* (San Francisco: Harper & Row, 1980).

2. See for instance E. Brooks Holifield, *A History of Pastoral Care in America* (Nashville: Abingdon Press, 1983) and Allison Stokes, *Ministry After Freud* (New York: Pilgrim Press, 1985) for historical evaluations of the influence and in part triumph of psychological language over religious language in pastoral counseling.

3. Edgar Draper, George G. Meyer, Jane Parzen, and Gene Samuelson, "On the Diagnostic Value of Religious Ideation" *Archives of General Psychiatry* (September 1965), Vol. 13, pp. 202-7.

4. Paul W. Pruyser, *The Minister as Diagnostician* (Philadelphia: Westminster Press, 1976).

5. Wayne E. Oates, *Behind the Masks* (Philadelphia: Westminster Press, 1987).

6. Don Browning, *The Moral Context of Pastoral Care* (Philadelphia: Westminster Press, 1976).

4

Consultation, Referral, and Contracts

After her first interview with Edgar, Beth was fairly clear that she was going to offer him the opportunity of a time-limited counseling contract. She liked Edgar, thought that she could be of help to him, and thought that she had a clear enough understanding of what brought him to her in the first place. While there is a real place for instinct or "gut feelings" in our deciding to offer counseling to those who come to us, there are other criteria that should be satisfied.

Beth had much more to go on than her feelings in deciding to work with Edgar. Beth also had considerable information about Edgar which came as a result of their diagnostic conversation. During the conversation Beth kept notes which followed the outline discussed in the previous chapter. Beth made use of these notes to make a determination of her ability to help Edgar and whether Edgar was a good candidate for time-limited counseling. In reviewing her notes she asked herself five questions:

1. Did Edgar have a fairly clear articulated presenting problem or Focal Relational Problem?
2. Did Edgar demonstrate the ability of give-and-take

necessary to develop a flexible relationship and did
he have a history of such relationships in the past?

3. Did Edgar show some flexibility in his relationship
   with Beth during the diagnostic interview?
4. Did Edgar show that he had some psychological
   mindedness?
5. Was Edgar motivated for lasting change rather than
   merely symptom relief?

Answering at least four of these questions in the
affirmative indicated that Edgar was a good candidate
for working with Beth in counseling. (See chapter 2 for
a more detailed discussion of these criteria in time-
limited counseling.)

Edgar and Beth were able to agree on the definition of
the FRP. At first this definition was rather vague: Edgar
was feeling out of sorts. In their conversation they were
able to sharpen the definition of this presenting
problem. Edgar was feeling less enthusiasm for work
and with his leisure time. He was tired and had lost his
normal enthusiasm for food as well. Both his wife,
Madge, and some of his work mates had noticed some
changes in Edgar's usual mood.

The FRP was further clarified in the closing part of the
diagnostic conversation. Edgar has much in his life to
look toward. He has travel plans and family to visit in
his retirement. At the same time, Edgar has been
suffering from the strain of grief, or, as Beth has put it,
from saying good-bye. Edgar, in the latter part of his
mid-life, seems to be caught in a real dilemma. If he is to
commit himself to his work and family life, that will also
inevitably mean facing the loss of those things that he
so enjoys. The solution that Edgar came to in dealing
with this dilemma was to limit his investment of energy
in anything at all. This solution, of course, was only
partially helpful because family and work still expected
much from him and were desirous of his participation.

Besides, he just did not feel very good. There is no doubt as well, as Beth learned in her diagnostic interview, that Edgar's solution (that is, limited investment of energy in work and family life) was one that he had used for many years, beginning as a boy who moved from place to place and on occasion was left by his father as he met his own work obligations.

Edgar also showed promise in fulfilling the second and third criteria. He had much experience in the past of having and holding meaningful relationships both in the family and with peers. His ability to relate to Beth was clear. He was able to express his feelings with some ease and was able to enjoy the give and take of their fondness for Penn State University. Edgar also was able to show that criterion four was fulfilled. He has some psychological sophistication. He was able to agree with Beth that the psychological effect of being caught between hello and good-bye had taken its toll. Finally, Edgar did not want just a quick relief—a sort of aspirin for the headache—but wanted to be able to reach some sort of resolution to his problem. He wanted to enjoy his present and future, knowing full well the limitations that are inherent in being human. It must be noted that the FRP is always clarified and possibly amplified during the course of the counseling. As the pastor and the counselee engage in a relationship of give-and-take, more and more of the presenting problem will become more fully known.

Consultation

If Beth and Edgar had not been able to come to a clear definition of the FRP, or had Beth not felt so sure that Edgar had fulfilled the basic criteria for time-limited counseling, there are other resources available to help her make a decision about a counseling relationship.

Consultation is a valuable resource available to the pastor.

To *consult* is to seek advice, to deliberate, or to counsel. In counseling it has the function of both aiding and clarifying the diagnostic process and therefore facilitating the counseling process. Many pastoral counselors, particularly if they are part of a counseling or church staff, make consultation an ordinary part of the intake or diagnostic process. The consultation need not be used only when there is some problem in understanding the counselee or if there are some problems in the treatment process itself.

Unfortunately, however, the pastor in the local parish will not have standard consultation procedures built into his or her practice. Therefore the consultation is usually requested because of some problem either in diagnosis or the counseling process. In my own mind the consultation is most useful in developing an adequate diagnosis or clear FRP. It is therefore desirable for the counseling pastor to have some resource available for supervision and consultation. The resource can be other clergy or other helping persons.

When there is a problem in understanding a counselee, the consultation becomes useful when:

1. It is not clear to the pastor why the person comes for help at the present time. This question is often raised when the problem is a long-standing one that the person has lived with for some time without much hindrance. Why is the person coming for help now? What new situation in life makes this problem such that counseling is sought now?
2. The language that the counselee uses is not existentially familiar to the pastor. In other words, the problem is complicated by the attitudes and situations of the counselor. The reason for this problem may be cultural, religious, or even political. The pastor should

admit that there are people with whom he or she may
have a difficult time in developing empathy. There are
many associations that can inhibit the diagnostic
process. The inability to take the role of the other or to
take it with too much identification is a signal for the
pastor to obtain consultation.

3. The counseling process itself gets stuck, or the
process seems unclear in its direction and applica-
tion. In this case the counselee seems to make no
movement, produces little in the way of material for
pastoral conversation, or the counselor feels unable
to make much cordial interaction.

A consultation can help clarify these situations and
may offer the pastor a way to continue the counseling or
consider a referral.

Most resourceful pastors have a variety of consultative sources from their community. One major resource
for consultation is the medical community, particularly
psychiatrists. It is a mistake to assume that the
psychiatrist must also provide the counseling if a
psychiatrist is consulted. Many psychiatrists are willing
to act as a medical resource and deal with medical
diagnosis and intervention, leaving the counseling to
the pastor. If the pastor has any notion that there is a
medical problem, it is mandatory to consult a medical
specialist. What may appear to be depression can often
be the result of some organic problem that only a person
trained in medicine can diagnose. If the depression is
severe, medication may be prescribed and monitored
by the physician while the counseling is carried on by
the pastor. Of course, development of a collaborative
relationship with a psychiatrist is dependent upon the
professional ability to relate as colleagues and over-
come professional rivalries or prejudices.

The pastor should also have available non-medical
consultants such as social workers, learning disabilities

specialists, clinical psychologists, alcohol counselors, and vocational counselors. Social workers, in particular, are often a valuable resource for both consultation and referral. Many social workers with graduate degree education (M.S.W.) are trained not only in counseling but also in how to find and use community resources that may be available.

Probably one of the best sources for consultation is also one of the most overlooked. One of the best ways of facilitating regular consultations is to organize a clergy consultation group. This type of group might meet once or twice a month for an hour or so each time. I know of several groups of clergy that meet monthly for a brown-bag lunch to discuss counseling work and for help in diagnosis and other kinds of consultation. It might be standard procedure of a group for each pastor to present a new counseling case for a half-hour and then get the impressions of the group both for diagnosis and for helping with the course of counseling. The group may also ask participation, from time to time, of guests who offer their insight into particular counseling situations and make themselves known to the other clergy as possible referral and consultation resources. Such groups give the pastors support in their counseling and emotional support in a most difficult part of ministry.

Confidentiality is a must in any consultation. Often it is best not to identify the counselee discussed by anything other than a first name or even with a fictitious name. It is understood that the material discussed, and any material presented, such as verbatims or tape recordings, cannot be shared outside of the consultation group. It is not necessary that the counselee know that the pastor receives consultation in his or her counseling. This is a judgment call, and the pastor may want to let the counselee know that all areas of ministry are discussed with others in confidence and not just this particular course of counseling. It is necessary, however, that the counselee know when counseling sessions are tape recorded and shared in consultation. In this case the counselee needs to sign a release statement that would allow the recording of the counseling for consultative purposes. A release form can simply state that the counselee is aware that the sessions are taped and that the tapes are used for professional consultation with another professional and not for any other purpose. It is important to remember that the consultant is bound by the same rules of confidentiality as is the counselor.[1]

If the pastor consults with another pastor or other professional, the consultation can take at least three forms. First, the counselee can be sent to the work place of the consultant and interviewed there. This is most often the way medical consultations are handled. The consultant would then contact the pastor with the results of the consultation. Second, the pastor can accompany the counselee to the work place of the consultant and participate in the consultation process. Later the consultant and the pastor could discuss what can be done in the future to help the person. The third type of consultation is the discussion between the pastor and the consultant, much like in the consultation group, where the discussion about the counselee can lead to insights about the future. It is important to know ahead of time what financial arrangement the consultant expects before the counselee is sent to him or her. In the first two modes of consultation the counselee is responsible to the consultant for any fees or charges. In the third mode of consultation any charge is between the pastor and the consultant.

Some form of consultation is essential for every pastor who does even a modicum of counseling. If a pastor provides more than two or three hours a week to formal and structured counseling, then the responsible pastor will also have regular consultation and supervision. While it might be preferable for the pastor to consult with a person who specializes in counseling and who is credentialed, the valuable resource of brother and sister clergy should also not be overlooked.[2]

Referral

A referral is the directing of a counselee to another professional for further evaluation and treatment. By referring a counselee the pastor gives up only his or her counseling relationship with the person. Other forms of ministry, including pastoral care, visitation, and teaching are not to be terminated. Only the formalized and limited counseling relationship is discontinued.

Probably the three most common reasons for referral are (1) the problem presented by the client is so complex or so far out of the experience and expertise of the pastor that adequate counseling would be difficult; (2) the pastor and the counselee have too much contact in other contexts that could compromise the counseling relationship; and (3) there is not enough time in the pastor's schedule to allow for adequate counseling, including time-limited counseling.

The first reason for a referral is usually easy to discern for most pastors who are interested in counseling. The most obvious example of this type of situation that may warrant referral is one of obvious psychosis which usually needs medical intervention. It is not necessary for the pastor to be a skilled diagnostician in severe and chronic psychological problems to be wary of attempting to enter into a counseling relationship with someone who has had repeated psychiatric hospitalizations, has visual or auditory hallucinations, or is paranoid in an extreme fashion. If there is any hesitation about how the person is describing the problem, referral is indicated. Of course, continued pastoral care is always appropriate.

Another type of problem that usually requires specialized intervention is chemical abuse, including alcoholism. Addiction to drugs, including alcohol, demands medical intervention and supervision. The withdrawal from alcohol can be fatal, for instance, if it is not medically supervised. In addition, alcoholism and other kinds of drug addiction are very resistant to individual counseling, particularly short-term counseling. If the pastor suspects drug or alcohol abuse, a referral to medical professionals is necessary. If the pastor takes the diagnostic interview seriously, then a history of drug and alcohol use will be discussed and referral can be effected. The problem of abuse may not become clear until the counseling process has already begun. Clergy are in a valuable position in being of most help in making this kind of referral.[3] Pastors should also be ready to refer to local Alcoholics Anonymous meetings.

The second reason for referral is probably the most common reason among most parish clergy. It is ill advised to attempt to counsel a person with whom there may be frequent contact outside the counseling relationship and normal functioning of the parish. This is to be avoided because the intimacy of the counseling relationship can be threatened if the counselee also has a persona to maintain which may be opposed to or in conflict with the material that is properly brought up in counseling. Some folks cannot be open and honest with their pastors because they feel that too much is expected of them or they want to protect the pastor from their reality. This admission may be more of a blow to the pastor's notions of omnipotence or to a narcissistic need to help all people, than it is damaging to the counselee's desire for help. As in other cases, if an ease in conversation about deep personal matters is not present, referral is clearly indicated. It might be difficult, for instance, for a clerk of session, or a chair of the church board, to confide in the pastor about marital infidelity and the like. The openness and acceptance that is necessary in building a counseling relationship would be compromised if such a dual relationship were to occur. In a similar manner, it would be most difficult, if not impossible, to do more than crisis intervention or pastoral care with a close friend or family member. Referral after hearing of the need of counseling, without even getting into the particulars, is best under these circumstances. Receiving consultation in these situations can make the decision to refer much more clear.

Another reason that familiarity with the potential counselee contraindicates counseling, and therefore may require referral, is the possible contamination of the transference that inevitably arises between the counselee and the counselor. While the dynamics of transference and countertransference will be discussed more fully in the next chapter, contact with a counselee outside of the counseling relationship can compromise and confuse the process of counseling. Generally the more common day-to-day contact between the pastor and a parishioner is not a problem. It is the more intense relationships, such as between pastor and secretary or board member, that can become confused. Many an attempt to provide intense pastoral counseling to someone too close in other relationships has ended in frustration or misunderstanding, often signified by much small talk during the session and missed counseling sessions by both the pastor and the counselee.

The last reason for referral is based upon the pragmatic realities of parish work. Unless the pastor is called to a parish ministry specifically to perform a counseling ministry, there is not enough time for more than a few counseling cases at any given time. Even if the pastor is called to full-time pastoral care, the counseling load can soon become filled, leaving little time for other pastoral duties such as visitation, crisis intervention, and education. It is for this reason that time-limited counseling is most attractive to the parish pastoral counselor. Even then time easily gets lost.

Finally, if a potential counselee does not fulfill the five criteria for time-limited counseling, and if possible consultation resources have been exhausted, referral should be considered. The first three criteria with the ability to articulate an FRP are the most important. Any four of the criteria should be filled with the first (the FRP) being absolutely necessary.

The referral works much like the consultation. The resourceful pastor will have a network of capable professionals, including pastoral counselors, able to take referrals of a special and of a general nature. Usually permission of the counselee to make a phone referral is all that is necessary. By this I mean that the pastor should have permission to call the referral source to find if the source will take the referral. If the answer is yes then the counselee is told to call and make his or her own appointment. It is best for the counselee to do this rather than having the pastor make the appointment. Counseling should always be voluntary. It is surprising how many people will feel obliged to follow a referral without any real motivation. Often it is to please the pastor. Persons who make their own calls place more of their own investment in the process. If the referral source is interested in the pastor's diagnostic formulations, then the pastor will need to have the written permission of the counselee to write such information in a letter to the referral source. Usually the referral source will communicate to the pastor if the counselee did in fact make contact. Of course the pastor can ask the counselee as well.

Because the issues of consultation and referral bring up issues of confidentiality and informed consent, it is necessary to make a comment or two about note taking and file keeping. It is best to keep all notes and files carefully locked, with access open to no one other than the pastor. It is best not to have files and ongoing case notes too long after counseling has been completed. A summary statement is all that is necessary. Too loose a handling of case notes—leading to some unauthorized person having access to information—can lead to a lawsuit or, more importantly, violated confidence. It is also unclear if the pastor performing counseling has the common law protection of the rights of confession. While the courts of most states recognize that what is said to clergy in terms of confession cannot be used in a court of law nor can the clergy be subpoenaed and questioned about information that may have been heard in confession or during priestly duties, it is not always clear that pastoral counseling fulfills the criteria of confession. The issue usually centers on the definition of who is clergy and what is priestly work. Some have argued that pastoral counseling is not confession and therefore is not immune from the law. Generally it is my understanding that if the counselee approaches the minister as a minister and requests counseling both of a psychological and religious nature, then the rights of confession do apply. If the counselor is only a counselor and does not necessarily identify him or herself as a religious worker sponsored by a religious body, then the rights of confession may not apply. No pastoral counselor can assume privileged treatment by secular authorities, and therefore he or she should be prudent in his or her record keeping, consulting, and referring practices. The law is not always consistent or fair. Note that secular psychotherapists have been shown not to have the right of privilege when subpoenaed for testimony concerning certain crimes.

Many states, such as Georgia, require that clergy who are told of possible child sexual or physical abuse inform the authorities for investigation. This is a wise and important law to uphold. Even if the investigation does not show that there was any abuse, it is always better to allow an investigation than to risk abuse of a defenseless child. States with such a law also protect the source of such information from legal retaliation.[4]

Contract Setting

While it may appear self-evident, the making of a counseling contract is dependent upon at least two preliminary steps. First, someone has actually asked for help from the pastor. Second, the counselee and the pastor have a clear idea of what the problem is through an understanding of the Focal Relationship Problem and how that problem affects others in the life of the counselee. Once this is established then a contract can be negotiated.

The contract for counseling should have six elements: time of appointment, length of the counseling "hour," place of the appointment, duration of counseling, a restatement of the FRP, and the cost, if any, of the counseling. All six elements of the contract must be very clear to both the counselee and the pastor.

The appointment is best remembered if it takes place on the same day of the week at the same time for a set amount of time, usually fifty minutes. While there can be some variation on time and day due to scheduling problems, they should be avoided. This agreement ritualizes the counseling experience, thereby underscoring the importance of the process: during a definite hour on the same day at a certain place the counselor and the counselee meet for a prescribed period of time to explore certain human problems. The contract is also set for the length of the counseling duration. For our purposes we have chosen ten sessions. It is important to make this element of the contract very clear. There will be ten sessions and only ten sessions. If the counseling takes fewer than ten sessions, fine, but there will not be any sessions beyond the tenth. If more counseling is needed, then referral should be discussed. With the time-limitation in mind, it is best to begin each session with a reminder of how many sessions are left in the contract. Likewise at the end of a counseling hour the pastor should make a verbal note of what session has just been completed and what number of sessions are left in the contract. Making these verbal notations at the beginning and end of each session gives both the counselee and the pastor some notion of control over the process and encourages the hard work of counseling.

Time-limited counseling is more effective than merely guessing about the amount of time available to the counselor. As many time-limited psychotherapy researchers have demonstrated, the issue of a closed course of counseling has great therapeutic power in and of itself, apart from just the convenience of the counselor. The most influential aspect of time-limited counseling is the anxiety that is provoked by the setting of an unalterable and definite termination date for the counseling. While many critics could wonder how useful anxiety is, and how ethical it is to artificially encourage it, anxiety does serve some useful function in the day-to-day life of most people. Most anxiety is a signal to beware of some potential problem or challenge. In animals it is a signal for fight or flight. It is in humans as well, but it is something more, for it is also a signal to face other problems. Anxiety is a state that has been described by several theological writers as being a warning signal for the person to be aware of his or her freedom, responsibility, and place in human relationships.

Not long ago a doctoral student took me to task about the merely negative notion of anxiety in time-limitation. This pastor of a Pentecostal urban church told me that hope for the end of suffering is good news and not necessarily felt as negative. This pastor went on to remind me that history is replete with stories of peoples who hoped for the end of suffering and oppression. In this sense the anxiety of time-limitation is good news not necessarily associated with feeling bad. The optimism that both the counselee and the pastor share about the possibility of growing encourages this liberating hope.

By limiting the duration of the counseling and focusing on the FRP, a pastor does make use of anxiety; but it is a type of anxiety that must be investigated for new ways of creating behaviors and situations that are more adaptable than those ways that have been used in the past. People come to counseling because the old ways no longer work and the anxiety and the feeling of suffering are no longer tolerable. Yet none of us has an unlimited amount of time at our disposal.

Finally the issue of fees should be discussed. For many pastors this is a touchy subject. While fees for service are normal for most practitioners, it has not been so obvious in parish work. I think that it is appropriate for the pastor to charge a sliding scale of fees for parish pastoral counseling. With the consent of the church governing board, the fees can be placed in the minister's discretionary fund, or the pastor may have some other place to put them. The church sees the pastor's counseling as part of the ministry for which the church does make a contribution in the pastor's salary. Pastoral counseling should be no different.[5]

Edgar arrived at Beth's office at the appointed time. Beth met him in her secretary's office. He had already helped himself to the coffee and Beth invited him into the office. After a few minutes of joining (always remember this important part of beginning any session) they had the following conversation.

Pastor:	Well, Edgar, how are things going in terms of what we decided to work on?
Edgar:	You mean the hello and good-bye?
Pastor:	Yeah. Have you given that some more thought?
Edgar:	Yes, I have. I told Madge about what you said, and she seemed to think that we were on to something. I agree. It seems that the sluggishness that I have been feeling is my being in between the two . . . which way do I go, sort of.
Pastor:	Yes. Would you like to spend some time talking about that?
Edgar:	Yes. What do you have in mind?
Pastor:	Well, I have been thinking quite a bit about it, too, and I would like to work with you over the next couple of months and see what we can come up with. What I have in mind is that we work with each other for ten sessions counting this one today. I can see you on Mondays at four-thirty. We can meet for fifty minutes each time. Let's keep mindful of how many sessions we have very carefully, and we will keep it to ten.
Edgar:	Well, do you think that ten is enough? I'm really not a mental case, of course, but is ten just a round number?
Pastor:	Well, ten is a nice round number, but more than that, I think that if we keep in mind our task, that ten sessions or even less is all that we will need. You seem ready to work on this and so am I.
Edgar:	Sounds right to me. I'm game.

Pastor:	Good. Now I want to give you this paper that will give you some idea of what pastoral counselors charge for counseling. I would like you to feel comfortable with making a commitment to pay into our deacon's fund for each of our ten sessions. If for some reason one of us misses a session, then we will continue counting the number of sessions with the next one. I will promise to give you at least a day's notice if I have to miss, and I hope you will do the same. How's that sound?
Edgar:	Yeah, I was going to ask you if I could make some kind of contribution. Madge and I talked about that, but we didn't know if you did that like a psychologist did, or what. This will be fine. Should I make the check out to the church?
Pastor:	That would be fine, and just put a notation on it that it is for the deacon's fund. Now, what we need to keep in mind—besides how much time we have in the counseling—is what we are working on.
Edgar:	Hello and good-bye and beat Ohio State!
Pastor:	You got it! This is session number one. Let's roll up our sleeves and get to it. . . .

Conclusion

In this chapter we have discussed how the pastor uses the material gathered in the diagnostic interview. The issue of counselee selection was discussed in terms of consultation and referral. In addition, the method of making a time-limited counseling contract was discussed. In the next chapter the process of time-limited counseling will be discussed paying particular attention to the issues of transference, countertransference, and interventions with the Focal Relational Problem.

Notes

1. The issue of confidentiality and privileged communication is a very important legal and ethical problem. For further reading on this subject see *The Journal of Pastoral Care* Vol. XXXIX, No. 4 (December 1983). In this issue there is a symposium on privileged communication with articles by psychologists, a lawyer, and a pastoral counselor. In addition see H. Newton Maloney, Thomas Needham, and Samuel Southard, *Clergy Malpractice* (Philadelphia: Westminster Press, 1986). See also William Harold Tiemann and John C. Bush, *The Right to Silence, Privileged Clergy Communication and the Law* (Nashville: Abingdon Press, Third Edition, 1989).

2. Often the pastor will have available pastoral counselors nearby who can provide supervision. Any pastoral counselor who is also a fellow or diplomat in the American Association of Pastoral Counselors is well trained and able to provide consultation. Of course many social workers, psychologists, and psychiatrists can also provide consultation.

3. For further information on alcohol and drug abuse see Howard Clinebell, *Understanding and Counseling the Alcoholic* (Nashville: Abingdon Press, 1968).

4. See note 1 above for a more detailed discussion of this issue.

5. For a more complete discussion of this important subject see John Patton, *Pastoral Counseling, A Ministry of the Church* (Nashville: Abingdon Press, 1983). See in particular chapter 3.

5

The Process of Time-limited Counseling

In this chapter the flow of a ten-session time-limited pastoral counseling process will be described and outlined. There are, however, several caveats to declare from the beginning. While this book attempts to offer the pastor a manual for doing time-limited pastoral counseling, most readers know that no systematic outlining of the counseling progression can rigidly contour the counseling process itself. This is particularly true when it comes to the content of the counseling dialogue. In most cases we look at each counseling relationship as a unique and discrete one. No two counseling relationships can or ought to be considered the same, either in content (such as in terms of the FRP or how the FRP is expressed) or in structure (when certain counseling techniques are applied).

One of the greatest compromises made by pastors in terms of their counseling is an inclination toward an overly rigidified reliance upon technique, at the expense of attending to the relationship that is before them. While people come to pastors because of their perception of the pastor's professional skill and spiritual accountability, they also come to them because of a feel for their authentic care and concern for human understanding and transformation. To rely too much on technique in a cookbook sort of way endangers the pastoral relationship and forces it far too much in the direction of the professional model, with all its problems as discussed in chapter 1. A major priority for the counselor is his or her attention to the ebb and flow of the relationship and not so much whether the pastor or counselee is fulfilling some kind of technical expectation. Every counselee is unique and will bring their own FRP. In like manner, each counseling relationship is unique in its dynamics and in its content. Counseling relationships are very complicated and are so because of transference and countertransference (to be discussed more fully in this chapter). Because of the unique quality of every counselee and each counseling relationship, the over reliance upon mere technique should be avoided.

It is not true, however, that the pastor can willy-nilly avoid structure in the counseling process. This is particularly true of time-limited counseling, in that this kind of counseling has a definite starting and ending time. Because the pastor and the counselee expect certain gains in the limited duration of the counseling relationship, certain structural devices are necessary. In fact, structure is dictated by the very nature of the time-limited contract, for the counseling takes place in a definite place for a definite period of time, and it attends to a specific area of interest (the FRP). Structure should not be seen as an inhibition to flow.

While this book can serve as a method and manual for parish pastoral counseling, it cannot serve the pastor as his or her only resource for fulfilling the counseling task. The pastor's accountability to both the governance of his or her faith tradition (from the local church and other arenas of ecclesiastical accountability) as well as to good counseling procedures must always be kept in bold relief. No counselor serves his or her counselees well without adequate consultation and supervision. It is irresponsible for the pastor to be involved in counseling without the additional counsel of peers and supervisors. Chapter 4 discusses this more fully. To take counseling seriously, accountability should be a priority, and this includes peer consultation and supervision. This book can offer a structure for encouraging supervision and consultation and should not be understood to supply the function itself.

General Principles

Four general principles should be attended to in each individual session. These principles are (1) the accounting and acknowledgment of the number of the particular counseling session, and the number left in the counseling contract; (2) joining at the beginning of each session; (3) the restatement of the FRP with any clarifications or alterations of it that have arisen from previous sessions; and (4) the activity of the counselor. It is essential that each of these principles be attended to as they contribute to the entire counseling process.

In time-limited counseling, time is a basic factor in what it is to be human. The human fact of finitude produces either an anxious longing for timelessness or an encouragement for action and hope. Is the counselee aware of the number of sessions that have transpired and that are left? Is there a sense of accomplishment in what has transpired? What is the counselee's reaction to the circumscribed number of sessions that are left? Of course, equally important are the feelings that the counselor has about the number and course of the counseling sessions. Is there a sense of progress and hope or is there some confusion about the process? If the latter is the case, careful attention to the process is important and can be useful for supervision and consultation.

Pastor:	(After Edgar settles into his chair) Hello, Edgar. This is session number two. We have just begun. After this session we will have eight more to go.
Edgar:	I liked the last time we met; it seems that maybe I've got some idea of where this might be going. I really don't know if eight more sessions is too much or too little, but let's get at it.
Pastor:	Well, eight is what we have—or nine counting today. Maybe you and I can tell what eight more means after we finish talking today. (The pastor notes to herself that she is uncertain what eight more sessions means to her as well and wonders what this feeling may indicate for her.)

What is important here is that the time limitation has something to do with both the counselee and the counselor. The issue of time within the relationship is an issue for both and will contribute to the continuing process.

Joining immediately follows the announcement of the number of the current session. In addition to reasons discussed as part of the intake interview, joining now reinforces the relational aspect of all pastoral counseling. Pastoral counseling is not the relationship between a professional and an objectified part of a person's personality or soul.[1] It is a human relationship based on mutual concern and experience. Of course the counselee comes to the pastor because he or she, in the counselee's mind, has special skills and interests in helping people. The counselee also comes because there is a sense that the pastor is more like him or her, as a counselee, than he or she is different. In addition, joining illustrates the mutual and shared process of counseling. The pastor as counselor and the counselee are in this thing together. Joining also validates aspects of the counselee's life that operate outside the realm of the counseling relationship and the FRP. The counselee is far more than just the reason that counseling is sought in the first place.

Pastor: I heard that storm three days ago really gave you power people a tough time.

Edgar: Well, not so much my team, but there were lines down all along the front as it passed up north of here a little ways.

Pastor: Oh, you got to sleep through the night then.

Edgar: Yeah, I got a call on my beeper when Madge and I were bowling. They just wanted me to be on alert, but I didn't have to go out.

Pastor: That's good. Say, you're taking up the lanes again, heh?

Edgar: Yeah, Madge is saying we should join the league again. Are you going to try bowling in the church league?

Pastor: Maybe. I don't help the average too much though.

Edgar: Well, it's for fun, isn't it? You don't bet on them, do you? (Said with a laugh)

Pastor: Only if it is against me! (Laugh)

Here the joining process not only solidifies the relationship and opens the pastor's interest in the counselee beyond the bounds of the counseling, it also gives the pastor some useful information. Edgar, in this instance, indicates that his recreational life is changing, which is one area of his life that he had found lacking in the diagnostic interview. In addition the pastor feels an ease in the relationship that was indicated by the friendly joking about her own bowling ability. Both of these bits of information gleaned from the joining are important indicators about the process of the counseling.

The third general principle of the counseling process is the reiteration of the FRP. Immediately after the accounting of the session number and joining, the counselor should restate the presenting problem as agreed upon in the diagnostic meeting. Time-limited counseling is problem-solving counseling, and it is essential to keep the focus of the problem in bold relief. To lose the focus of the counseling will doom it to failure. However, the FRP will more than likely alter or be refined as the counseling progresses. For that reason it is best for the counselor to relate the FRP as it was discussed in the previous session and ask the counselee how it has been addressed or observed during the time between the last and current session. Many times the FRP is discussed in a short-hand way. In the counseling relationship between Edgar and Beth, the FRP was described as "saying hello and good-bye." This short-hand phrase denoted, to both Edgar and Beth, Edgar's way of confronting his anxiety about investing energy in enjoyable activities that he could lose. In a sense the phrase signifies Edgar's anticipatory grief that tends to inhibit his present ability to derive satisfaction in work and personal relationships. Such short-hand phrases should always be clearly agreed upon by both the counselor and the counselee probably from the diagnostic session but surely from the first actual counseling session.

Pastor: Last time we met we talked about hello and good-bye in a few ways, such as when you grew up in an Army family; how it worked with things on the job; and how it worked with the girls and their new families. I wonder if you have been giving any more thought to hello and good-bye in other ways.

Edgar: (Silence for a moment) Well . . . yes, I guess that I have. One way that it seems that I think about hello and good-bye is these days with Madge and simple things like bowling and stuff like that. (Silence)

Pastor: Say more about that.
Edgar: I don't know what to say really. I mean, I'm not sure what the angle is on that. It just seems that something is there.
Pastor: There's something there with hello and good-bye with Madge, but you aren't really sure what that could be. It's just that something is there.
Edgar: (Silence) Yeah. Maybe now that the girls are out of the house. I don't know.
Pastor: Well, Edgar, maybe you could think of what it is that you are saying hello and maybe good-bye to in terms of that . . . I mean now that you and Madge are alone again with the kids grown and out of the house.
Edgar: You mean that I am saying hello and good-bye to Madge? Hmm . . . It is a different kind of relationship now, that is for sure.
Pastor: Well, let's name that different kind of relationship. What kind of way are you shaky about saying hello to that?

The final principle, which should always be tended, is the activity of the counselor. In many ways the prescribed duration of the counseling relationship and the focusing on the presenting problem or FRP demands the very active participation of the counselor in keeping the goals of the counseling clear. In problem-solving, time-limited counseling there is no time for the counselor to remain passive. This does not mean that silence cannot be appropriate under some circumstances. Silence on the part of the counselor and the counselee does not always mean inactivity. Often the making of connections of strains of the FRP in the relational life of the counselee takes some silent work.

In my own clinical practice careful observation of the counselee during silences is quite helpful. It has been my experience that when a client is working through a thought in silence he or she will often avert his or her eyes to one side or the other. This will be held sometimes for several moments and often indicates very serious thinking activity. I let this go in silence. When the counselee's eyes return to focusing more directly and usually in my direction, I then assume that the thinking is done and I will ask the counselee what he or she was thinking. Sometimes I will ask the question with: "Where were you just now? What were you thinking?"

Nonetheless it is essential that the counselor be helpfully active in the process. When in doubt about silence, it is always helpful to bring the subject back to the issue of the FRP.

Pastor:	(After a silence of two minutes or so) Edgar, it looked like you were thinking about something just now. Can you share it?
Edgar:	I'm not sure what it was I was thinking. It has something to do with not being able to bowl forever. Sounds kind of silly, doesn't it?
Pastor:	Silly? I am not sure what you mean.
Edgar:	(Silence for two more minutes) Well . . . I am not sure what that means. (More silence)
Pastor:	Tell me about how you feel about bowling and how hello and good-bye may have something to do with that.
Edgar:	Well, it is something that Madge and I have loved to do with each other and with the gang. I guess there is something that isn't there. I mean hello and good-bye and something I love.
Pastor:	I should think so. Let's talk more about that.

If the pastor keeps in mind and uses each of the four principles outlined above, the flow of the counseling relationship is more assured. The four principles reinforce the time limitation of the counseling relationship; facilitate the cooperative nature of the counseling endeavor; keep the focus of the counseling clear; and demand the activity (including the observational activity) of the counselor.

The Fields of Attention in the Process of the Counseling

Obviously the process of counseling cannot rest alone with the force of the general principles described above. As important as they are, they are basically starting points or building blocks upon which the rest of the course of counseling depends. In his book *Principles of Psychoanalytic Psychotherapy*, Lester Luborsky describes an important element that rests upon these building blocks.[2] This element is the attending to the FRP (called the Core Conflictual Relationship Theme by Luborsky) as it is acted out in three fields (or spheres) in the life of the counselee. These three fields are: (1) the FRP as it has been experienced in the counselee's past; (2) the FRP as it is experienced in the here-and-now relationships outside of the counseling relationship; and (3) the FRP as it is experienced within the counseling relationship, that is, as it is enacted in the relationship with the pastor. By exploring each of these fields of enactment of the FRP, the counselee's understanding is facilitated and the process of counseling proceeds to its goal.

The first field is relatively obvious and more than likely will be discussed at least in an indirect way during the diagnostic interview. After the FRP has been established both in short-hand and in detail, the counselee should be encouraged to recount how it occurred in relationships in the past. Particularly of importance is how it was experienced with highly significant persons such as parents, siblings, other relatives, spouses, workmates, and friends. The FRP was developed in the counselee's past as a way to deal with anxiety and conflict. This way of adaptation then is assumed in other relationships where it may not be as satisfying an adaptation, if ever it was in the first place.

The second field is where the counselee is encouraged to take a look at how the FRP is operating in the present with important relationships. These experiences can be elicited, often, during the early part of each counseling session after the naming of the session, joining, and the restatement of the FRP.

Pastor: Tell me, Edgar, how are things at work these days? How are you getting along with your friend, the supervisor?

Edgar: Things are going along O.K. usually. I'm still embarrassed with how I yelled at him a few weeks ago, except I don't think that he thinks about it so much.

Pastor: What do you mean by embarrassed?

Edgar: Well, you know, I sort of lost it with him. I mean he is an old friend of mine and not just a boss. I guess that there was no call for me to snap at him.

Pastor: I don't know if there was no call or not, Edgar. I am wondering, though, if there is anything to do with hello and good-bye with that feeling you have.

Edgar: Yeah, I did think of that. It is like . . . well . . . if I stay embarrassed, then I don't deal with him. Sort of like . . . well, then if I don't have anything to do with him, nothing is gained but nothing is lost either.

Pastor: Is that true? That doesn't change the fact that you must deal with him or the fact that you are friends, does it?

Edgar: No, I work with him and we used to even take family vacations together. We go way back. Same old stuff here, too, I guess.

Pastor: Sure looks like it, doesn't it?

Finally, the third field takes into account the experience of the FRP as it is enacted in the relationship between the pastor and the counselee. Attending to this field can be difficult at times, to be sure. One reason for this is the discomfort that may be felt in dealing face to face with a relationship. In a sense, a kind of modesty can be at play here. Another reason is that the subtlety of transference and countertransference (to be discussed more fully later in this chapter) can hinder dealing with this important field. It is with this kind of material that supervision and consultation can be most helpful. Attending to this field places a demand on the pastor to monitor his or her own feelings always in relationship to how the FRP is understood and being experienced. It is important for the counselor to be aware that the time-limited duration imposed by the counseling contract will often encourage the enactment of the FRP in the counseling field.

Edgar:	Are you sure that ten sessions are enough?
Pastor:	I'm not sure what you are asking right now.
Edgar:	Well, it seems that we are just getting started and you remind me that we only have four sessions left. Maybe we ought to just quit now and not waste our time.
Pastor:	Hello and good-bye again?
Edgar:	What do you mean?
Pastor:	It seems that you have been enjoying and getting something out of our conversations. When I reminded you that we are over halfway through our contract, you want to stop now.
Edgar:	Yeah, I guess you are right. I want to stop now rather than see it end. Yeah, I see what you mean. That doesn't mean that I like it.
Pastor:	Well, why does that mean that you can't enjoy what we have now and what we will have in another way? I am your pastor even when this is done.
Edgar:	Yes, that is true. It did sound as if I was willing to let that go, too. Same old stuff there, too.

Pastor: Sounds as if that is something important to keep in mind. It happens in other ways, too, say at work or home.

In this example, the pastor, Beth, was able to make use of how the FRP was being played out in the counseling relationship. She used the FRP short-hand and directly related it to the relationship she had with Edgar. In addition, she was able to relate this to other fields of the FRP as it related to Edgar. Each of the three fields of the enactment of the FRP should be attended to in each session. There can be a flow from one field to another, and doing this, according to Luborsky, allows the counselee to achieve an expanded view of the problem and take ownership of it. In addition, attending to the FRP as it occurs in the third field, which is the one in the counseling relationship, often yields the most helpful therapeutic value. This is because there is a sense of control that is possible, because events are happening in the here and now.[3] It is also useful for the counselor to relate how the three fields have been discussed in past sessions and how those discussions affect the discussion in the current session.[4]

Transference and Countertransference

Transference and countertransference are phenomena that occur in virtually every counseling relationship. In most cases they are also phenomena that are not well understood by most inexperienced counselors, and subsequently there is quite a mystique built up about them. It is not my intention to describe fully the two phenomena. There is a great body of literature available to interested readers.[5] In addition, the issues of transference and countertransference are best dealt with in the supervision and consultation process. In those relationships an understanding of the phenomena really comes to life. My purpose in discussing them at all is to alert the pastor to their significance and possible uses, particularly as they arise in relationship to the ubiquitous FRP.

According to Hinsie and Campbell, transference is

in psychoanalytic therapy, the phenomenon of projection of feelings, thoughts, and wishes onto the analyst, who has come to represent an object from the patient's past. The analyst is reacted to as though he were someone from the patient's past; such reactions, while they may have been appropriate to the conditions that prevailed in the patient's previous life, are inappropriate and anachronistic when applied to an object (the analyst) in the present.[6]

This definition has at least two assumptions. First, transference is the repetition of past significant relationship patterns in a new context such as the counseling relationship. The unfolding of the transference occurs spontaneously and is an attempt to relive past experiences. Usually this unfolds beyond the consciousness of the counselee. It is up to the observational ability of the counselor to point this out. In terms of the FRP this observation is usually obvious and can be kept in mind as it arises in an analysis of the FRP in the third field of the counseling process.

Second, most classical understandings of transference hold that it is pathological, which is to say, it is a vestige of maladaptive behavior. In terms of an FRP this may in fact be the case, but transference need not always be seen as maladaptive. Langs has argued that transference is best understood as a rather broad phenomenon with many colorations. These colorations can include the revival of past experiences, impulses, fantasies, and conflicts in the relationship in the here and now with the counselor all the way to a necessary component of establishing a therapeutic alliance (not unlike the give-and-take in the relationship described in chapter 3). Therefore, this kind of transference is a necessary ingredient for selection of a counselee for time-limited counseling.[7] Besides telling the counselor about how the counselee may handle anxiety and the FRP, transference can also give the counselor some idea of the therapeutic alliance. Recently, clinical theoreticians have been inclined toward describing all feelings the counselee has about the counselor within the realm of transference. For this reason, warm and friendly feelings and cooperative feelings can be considered transference reactions.

Warm and friendly feelings may not just be caused by the scintillating personality of the counselor alone. Positive feelings can occur because the client has a trust in the pastor's professional ability and even in her or his moral authority. The counselee may feel positively because he or she is now in the hands of a known healer and the hope of relief for long developed daily problems may be near. It is important that the pastor interpret this type of transference for what it is: confidence in the relationship and hope for the counselee's own motivation for change.

Transference phenomena will often occur during the rise of anxiety in the counselee when the FRP is being directly experienced or confronted. As the FRP issues are confronted or pointed out by the counselor, it is not unusual for the FRP in the third field to come into play. The counselor needs to be well aware of this. Every time that transference seems to occur, the counselor must describe it to the counselee and describe it in relation to the FRP. The reason that transference must be described is that often the transference is a way the counselee enacts the FRP. Transference can also be a way of putting on the counselor expectations that allow the counselee an opportunity to avoid his or her own responsibility for living his or her own life. The above case vignette illustrating the FRP in the third field is also an example of Beth interpreting a transference reaction. Here Beth pointed out that Edgar wanted to divest himself of the therapeutic alliance rather than face the saying of good-bye to a satisfying relationship, even though the relationship would continue in a different context.

It must also be seen that transference can prick the emotional experience of the counselor. Part of the response of the counselee may stimulate the counselor's own countertransference.

According to Hinsie and Campbell, countertransference is defined as

> the effects on his understanding or technique of the analyst's unconscious needs and conflicts. The patient's personality, or the material that he produces, or the analytic situation as such represents an object from the analyst's past, onto which past feelings and wishes are projected. A broader definition would include not only situations in which the patient serves as a real object onto whom something is transferred, but also those where the patient serves merely as a tool to gratify some need of the analyst, such as alleviation of anxiety or mastery of guilt feelings.[8]

In short, countertransference can be seen as the counselor's transference.[9] Just as with the counselee's transference, countertransference on the part of the counselor need not be seen as necessarily pathological or maladaptive. It can be argued that countertransference is a necessary ingredient for the development of empathy.[10] Countertransference is a necessary part of counseling in that a counselor's often unconscious perceptions and understandings of the counselee come about by means of partially short-lived identifications with the counselee. At the same time, it is important that the counselor not rest with this identification, for it is the counselor's responsibility to then swing back to the objective role of interpreter and counselor rather than as pure identifier.

It is often difficult to know about countertransference unless the counselor has a supervisor or peer consultation group that is interested not only in the counseling productions of the counselee, but also in how the counselor is feeling about the counselee and the process of the counseling. While it may be fairly easy to observe the goings on in the counselee and in his or her social life, work life, historical life, and family life, it is most difficult for the counselor to be able to offer the same observational stance on him or herself as counselor in relation to the counselee in the counseling process. To put it most analytically, it may be difficult—if not, for some, impossible—to be both subject and object at the same time. To be observer of the counselee and the counseling process is one thing, but to also be an observer of the counselor as a self in the process and therefore also be the subject is a most difficult mission. It is with this situation that the supervisor and consultation group can be most useful. In addition, it is most helpful if the counselor has had some personal counseling either in the past or concurrently with doing counseling so that there is some sensitivity to the counselor's own FRP and how it can impinge on the relationship with the counselee. The advice here is: Counselor, know thyself!

Edgar: I just don't know about this. I mean, I had a real good thing going with Frank (Frank was the pastor who was at the church before Beth arrived), especially when my dad died. He retired and went to Florida not long after that.

Pastor: You are wondering about the limited time we have in counseling and whether I can do you any good. I am sure that we can work together because we have done well before now and besides, we are going to have a relationship after the counseling is over. Like I said, I will still be your pastor. I also plan to be around this church and town for some time.

Edgar: You said there are no guarantees about those things, didn't you? I mean, that I should be able to enjoy what I have and what I can have.

Pastor: Yes, Edgar, I did say that. (Silence as Edgar looks directly at Beth as she quietly surveys her own feelings and emotions) You know, Edgar, I'm feeling something about the hello and good-bye thing myself. I felt very defensive when you were talking about Frank, and at the same time I wanted to make you feel better when you were expressing some disappointment about the counseling. I wonder what that has to do with your hellos and good-byes?

Edgar: Well, I like this, and I don't like thinking we only have a few sessions left.

Pastor: Yes, and I like it, too, but we have a contract. That is all we really need in order to deal with what brought you in to see me in counseling. You know if we both allowed ourselves to change the deal, we would avoid dealing with hello and good-bye, wouldn't we?

Edgar: You have a point there. . . .

What seemed to have occurred in this segment of the counseling is that Edgar was again expressing the FRP, this time in the third field. His anxiety about ending an enjoyable relationship seemed also to tap into Beth's need to be the rescuer. At the same time, it tapped into her own feelings of insecurity in being compared to her senior predecessor at the church. Beth's countertrans-ference almost got the best of her, and she even had fleeting thoughts of extending the counseling contract. Luckily, because of her supervision and own therapy (that dealt with her own grandiosity and need to be needed) she was able to monitor her feelings and make a recovery to the third field of Edgar's expression of the FRP.

Of the three fields of the expression of the FRP, it is within the third field that the issues of transference and countertransference are the most important, but they are often also the issues of neglect by counselors.

> This neglect is especially unfortunate since the patient-therapist relationship is potentially the most profitable arena because it is where the "tests" of the relationship are carried out and need to be observed. When the tests are passed and understood, special power is conferred upon the patient through his or her having "confronted the lion" by learning about the central relationship problems by direct and immediate observation in the here and now.[11]

As difficult as it may be, it is essential that the issues of transference and countertransference be dealt with head on. Again, it is important that the counselor use supervision and consultation in dealing with this delicate but beneficial aspect of the counseling process.

The Stages of the Time-Limited Process

A ten-session time-limited counseling process can be divided into three stages. There is the opening game; the middle game; and the end game.[12] While it is important that the counselor allow each counseling experience to be what it is and that is unique and new, my own experience is that each time-limited counseling process follows certain general stages.

The first stage, or opening game, usually is one of

great energy and excitement in the prospects of the helpfulness of the counseling. This stage usually consists of the first three or four sessions. What some counselors would call a "flight into health" and therefore artificial is in my own experience usually a manifestation of real progress and interest on the part of the counselee for making lasting change and the excitement that arises from obtaining insight. This enthusiasm is usually infectious and therefore encourages the excitement of the counselor (a form of countertransference). The excitement of the counselee produces a feedback loop that feeds the excitement of the counselor, which in turn feeds again the excitement of the counselee. This stage is necessary for the maintenance of the therapeutic alliance and will offer the fuel to keep the engines burning during the second stage: the middle game. If there is no excitement in the opening game, there should be concern that the FRP has not been sufficiently described and agreed upon by both the counselee and counselor.

The middle game, usually the fourth through the seventh or eighth sessions, is usually experienced as a waning of excitement, but almost paradoxically this stage is where the most important work of the counseling takes place. It is during the middle game that the FRP shows itself to be most prevalent and even intractable. It is also in the middle game that the FRP is most often expressed in one of the three fields with more regularity than other fields. The counselor needs to be most careful to relate the field being expressed to the other two fields. It is during this stage, when the romance has worn off, that the counselee can achieve some mastery of the FRP and in fact learns to be his or her own counselor. The FRP no longer is experienced as something new, in part because of the redundancy of its interpretation by the counselor. It is through this redundancy, however, that the counselee achieves mastery over the FRP and achieves the ability to look to the future. Great care should be taken by the counselor during the middle game for there not to be too premature a termination of the counseling. While the counseling contract does not allow for an extension of the number of sessions, it does allow for fewer than ten sessions. The desire for a termination during the doldrums of the middle game should be resisted just enough to see how the desire functions within the fields of the FRP. It could be that mastery has been achieved and a termination can be considered. Even if a termination is agreed upon, and it turns out to be premature, the sessions left in the original contract can still be used, and the termination should be with that provision clearly stated. Again, supervision can be helpful in making this determination. During the middle game the fantasy of extending the counseling beyond the contracted ten sessions is often expressed.

The end game, usually the last two or three sessions, is the process of facing the issue of time head on. The counseling will end and the end is in sight. This is underscored in each session as the counselor reminds the counselee of the number of the current session and the number left in the contract. The most important part that the counselor plays in the end game is handing over the counseling responsibility to the counselee him or herself. One of the goals of pastoral counseling is helping people to help themselves. This is done by the counselor's making interpretations of the three fields as they have related to material that has been brought up in the previous seven or so sessions. The redundancy of interpretation of the various expressions of the FRP leads to mastery.

In each of the stages there are certain ways that the counselor should be attentive to expressions given by

116

the counselee. It is best to keep in mind a three-part pattern in the expressive technique. First, the counselor should attempt to suspend any predetermined idea of what the counselee is going to say. This is an attitude of openness to what the counselee is saying by allowing it to be taken in on its own terms. The second part is for the counselor to attempt to weave what has been said into how it may apply to the FRP in one or all of the three fields of the FRP's expression. Third, the counselor should carefully relate to the counselee an interpretation. Timing is essential in this three-part process. Too quick an interpretation could cut off the experience of expression by the counselee. Too hesitant a response could indicate unclarity on the part of the counselor on what has been said; of course, counter-transference could also be a factor. After listening with the suspension of expectation, the counselor allows the next two parts to relate to the FRP. A very important part—particularly during the end game—is allowing enough time for the counselee to come to his or her own conclusions. At any rate, when an interpretation is made, the counselor should return to the listening with a suspension of judgment, and so the cycle goes.[13]

(The following conversation took place during the eighth session.)

Edgar: We are planning a trip to see Cindy in California. I'm really looking forward to it, seeing the kids and the grandbabies and all. I love that California sun.

Pastor: (Silence) So you are looking forward to the trip.

Edgar: Yes, I am, and Madge is excited, too. I always dread vacations. All the planning, and then you get there, and then it is time to go home again.

Pastor: So there are mixed feelings—good and not so good.

Edgar: Yes, Beth, that is right. (Silence) Hello and good-bye, you might say.

Pastor: Sounds like you know what it is about. Will that get in the way of you and the kids and the grandchildren?

Edgar: It could, but I don't think so. Why make what is a good thing a burden?

Pastor: Sounds like you are going to make sure that doesn't happen.

Edgar: Right. Hey, I heard that you were going to bowl again in the league. Is that true?

Pastor: I have given that some thought. Think you will have me?

Edgar: Sure. We need some novices in the league, too.

Pastor: I'm still interested in how you feel about the trip. You really feel you are on top of that and the hello and good-bye thing?

Edgar: Yes, I do, and also how that plays into all sorts of things.

Pastor: Even in our relationship.

Edgar: Yeah, even in that.

Here Beth has listened to the expression made by Edgar and then waited to make an interpretation in terms of the FRP. In this case Edgar beat her to it as could be expected in the end game of a successful counseling process. Even though Edgar had made his own interpretation, Beth listened again to a change of subject and returned the subject to the FRP expression that was made previously. Edgar's response assured her that the process had gone well.

Conclusion

In addition to the value of supervision and peer consultation, time-limited pastoral counseling moves through definite stages. Throughout these stages the FRP is observed in the three fields of its enactment. All the while, the phenomena of transference and countertransference should be noted.

In the final chapter, the issue of termination of the counseling relationship will be discussed, and the conclusions that can be made as a result of a short-term parish pastoral counseling relationship.

Notes

1. For a more detailed discussion of the healing aspects of the pastoral relationship see John Patton, *Pastoral Counseling: A Ministry of the Church* (Nashville: Abingdon Press, 1983), chapter 7.

2. Lester Luborsky, *Principles of Psychoanalytic Psychotherapy, A Manual for a Supportive-Expressive Treatment* (New York: Basic Books, 1984). See especially chapter 7, "Expressive Techniques: Listening and Understanding," pp. 90ff.

3. Ibid., pp. 110-12.

4. Ibid., p. 113.

5. See for instance the massive two volume work by Robert Langs, *The Therapeutic Interaction* (New York: Jason Aronson, 1976). This work annotates the literature on the subject in the first volume and in the second Langs offers his own synthesis of the various theories. The interested reader can also refer to the index of virtually any text on counseling or psychotherapy to get a commentary on the phenomena.

6. Leland E. Hinsie and Robert Jean Campbell, *Psychiatric Dictionary*, Fourth Ed. (New York: Oxford University Press, 1976), pp. 780-81.

7. Langs, *The Therapeutic Interaction*, Vol. 2, pp. 178-79.

8. Hinsie and Campbell, *Psychiatric Dictionary*, p. 167.

9. See Langs, *The Therapeutic Interaction*, for a more detailed discussion.

10. For a very fine discussion of the role of countertransference and the process of empathy see Rollo May, *The Art of Counseling* (Nashville: Abingdon Press, 1967), chapter 3.

11. Luborsky, *Principles of Psychoanalytic Psychotherapy*, p. 127.

12. For another perspective on this stage sequence of time-limited counseling see James Paul Gustafson, *The Complex Secret of Brief Psychotherapy* (New York: W. W. Norton, 1986).

13. See Luborsky, *Principles of Psychoanalytic Psychotherapy*, chapter 7.

6

Endings and Conclusions

Time-limited counseling, as I have proposed it, understands the ending of the counseling process in very definite and clear-cut ways. Unlike open-ended, so called long-term counseling, the kind of counseling proposed in this book focuses on problem solving through an understanding of the FRP in the three fields of activity (see the previous chapter). It also takes seriously the limitation of the duration of the counseling contract. After an FRP has been agreed upon by the counselor and the counselee, a contract is made to address it for ten sessions. The counselor and the counselee may take fewer than ten sessions to complete the process but they will *never* take more than ten sessions. More often than not, a ten-session limitation does not create a problem for those persons who are suitably selected for the process. The diagnostic criteria outlined in chapter 4 help to ensure the correct selection of the proper counselees best suited for time-limited counseling. Referral to another counselor after the course of a ten-session process—if that is indicated —is always a possibility.

Counselors and counselees take termination of the counseling seriously because the first goal of pastoral counseling is perceived as achievable: pastoral counseling helps people help themselves. In most cases by the ending part of the counseling there has been sufficient repetition of the FRP that the counselee begins to observe him or herself in the behaviors that created the impetus for counseling in the first place. The counselee is now ready to go it alone, and though there may be some hesitation in anticipating the ending of counseling, in most cases enough control over the presenting problem is achieved. The counselor also may have hesitations about the termination because the counselor must also face her or his own ambivalence about the limitation of time. The ending of the counseling should always be seen as a cooperative effort, just as the rest of the counseling process is.

In time-limited counseling, dealing with termination of the counseling is built in from the very beginning. This is done every session, from session one to ten, in the beginning and end of every individual session. The session number is announced at the beginning (after the all-important joining and just before the restatement of the FRP), and the counselee is reminded of the number of sessions left in the contract. Each session also is ended with a reminder of the number of sessions that have transpired and the number that are left. This important aspect of the structure of time-limited counseling helps prepare both the counselor and the counselee for the termination of the counseling contract.

Termination also is handled by the counselor with the counselee during the middle phase of the counseling. It is during the middle phase and into the ending phase that the counselor serves the counselee by pointing out important events that have occurred during the course of the counseling when the counselee has successfully monitored and confronted an aspect of the FRP in one of the three fields of investigation (the

FRP in the counselee's history; in the present outside of the counseling; and in the counseling relationship itself). By recognizing that the FRP has been confronted, the counselee and the counselor can see that the end of counseling is appropriate, even though problems of life can and will continue. The pastor reinforces that the counselee can face subsequent problems, especially dealing with the FRP, with greater facility.

Another important aspect of termination has already been discussed in the previous chapter. According to Luborsky, the counselee or the counselor "may lose hope of ever achieving goals and arriving at termination. In this case, one party . . . may show a premature inclination to stop treatment. It is recommended that the therapist consider ways of dealing with such inclinations, especially through understanding the transference."[1] More than likely, an issue of transference or countertransference is always playing a role in such a desire for a premature termination. It is essential for the counselor to monitor his or her own feelings about ending and to investigate with the counselee how the desire for premature termination plays a role in the FRP as expressed in the counseling relationship. This must take into consideration the issues of transference and countertransference.

Finally, the ending of counseling brings to the forefront the issue of whether the successes in dealing with the FRP during the counseling process will be maintained after the counseling is over. This issue also brings up the question of further contact or extending the counseling contract.[2] In the first case it is important to underscore with the counselee that dealing with the FRP during the counseling process is but a rehearsal for dealing with it outside the counseling process, including when the counseling is over. Unrealistic expectations that all problems will be solved—much less that the FRP will be completely banished—should be pointed out. Problems will continue, so it is essential to communicate to the counselee that one is preparing to play the role of counselor for him or herself. This is one meaning of the first goal of pastoral counseling: helping people to help themselves. Any plea to extend counseling beyond the original contract should be handled firmly and with empathy, because endings are difficult for counselors as well.

Further contact between the counselor and the counselee in a parish setting is expected and, in the life of a parish, encouraged. It goes without saying that the pastor does not abdicate the ministry of pastoral care just because a pastoral counseling contract has been completed. Other kinds of ministry are not ended: e.g., teaching, organizing, and shepherding (to use Hiltner's categories). The pastor and the counselee/parishioner may even, from time to time, briefly discuss and recall the counseling process, with a mention of the FRP or by sharing subjects that were shared in the joining process. This kind of contact not only signals the ongoing relationship between pastor and congregant, but it also reinforces the importance of the intimacy of the counseling process. It was and is special.

Though the counseling contract is set for ten sessions, there can be some accommodation for one additional session. It is often my own practice to allow a follow-up counseling session after the end of a ten-session counseling process. This follow-up session is introduced in the last session. The counselee is told that if he or she would like, in three months an appointment is appropriate to review how things are going in terms of the FRP. The initiative for such a follow-up appointment is left to the counselee. I then let the counselee know that if further counseling is needed, either with the original FRP or with another problem, then a referral will be made to an appropriate resource in the community. Further counseling with the pastor should be discouraged, though there could be some circumstances, rarely, that the pastor may want to enter into another counseling contract. This follow-up gives the counselee the opportunity to have some time to act as self-counselor and the opportunity to reinforce this self-help through reporting it to the pastor. As optional as it is, expectations for the follow-up session must be set forth carefully. Needless to say, emergency calls or crisis situations should be handled on their own merits, just as in any crisis situation, whether the person or persons had been in counseling or not. The pastor's supervisor or supervisors should be of help in discerning what is related to counseling and what is not.

The actual structure of the last session is fairly simple. The counselor first joins, numbers the session, and restates the FRP. Following this ritual the counselor gives a brief review of the entire counseling process by describing the diagnostic session, the uncovering of the FRP, and how the FRP was investigated within the three fields. Special emphasis is placed upon the successful ways that the counselee has dealt with the FRP, and these are underscored and pointed out as useful for the future. This kind of reminiscence of the process with its success and rough spots is carried out in a dialogue with the counselee. Both the counselor and the counselee therefore share in retelling the narrative of the counseling process. The counselee should be encouraged to add to, clarify, and challenge the counselor's retelling of the story. After the recounting of the counseling process and the role that all players have had in it, the counselor then discusses with the counselee the follow-up session. The session can then end with an extended period of joining talk, what I call social leave-taking, that marks the ending of the counseling and the beginning of a different kind of future relationship. The following verbatim account between Beth and Edgar illustrates a final session.

Pastor: So, Edgar, I have made a decision.

Edgar: What do you mean?

Pastor: I am going to stick to cheering for Penn State football and give up trying to be a league bowler. Penn State not only has more luck, but has more skill to cheer about.

Edgar: Yes, I heard that your team didn't do so well in the beginners division. We bowled Friday night, and they were talking about you all. Maybe you are right, but it isn't winning that is the fun of it all, really—not that it isn't nice. Say, maybe I could bowl on your team as a ringer.

Pastor: Right, Edgar, like nobody would notice you.

Edgar: Well, maybe I could grow a beard.

Pastor: Hmm. Maybe we should give that some thought. (A moment of silence) Edgar, this is session number ten, and our last session.

Edgar: That is hard to believe. It seems that we just started these talks. It has been good though.

Pastor: Yes, I think that they have. . . .

Edgar: (Interrupting) Sometimes I don't know if we have done what we wanted to do, though.

Pastor: (Ignoring the implicit plea for additional sessions) Well, why don't we take a look at what has happened?

Edgar: O.K.

Pastor: I remember you coming to me that Sunday after church. You seemed really hesitant to talk to me, but it seemed that you had something to say.

Edgar: I didn't know what to say, but you let me say whatever I wanted. I appreciated you for that.

Pastor: We made an appointment to talk without the rush of getting home from church, and we talked about some important things. One of the most important things we talked about was what was happening in your life, like changes at work, the girls marrying and leaving home and having their own families, and some concerns you and Madge had about your feeling sluggish and out of sorts. We also talked about some things that you had and continue to have some strong feelings about. I mean things such as your relationship with your dad, who was often away from the family, your relationship with your sisters, your relationship with Madge, the deaths of both your mom and dad when they were living with you, and your anticipation of retirement and what to do with yourself after you were finished with work. Right so far?

Edgar: So far, so good. Then we started talking about hello and good-bye.

Pastor: Right. That is something that we talked about every time we got together. Hello and good-bye. That meant something about how you reacted to things and relationships that you enjoyed and looked forward to, but were sometimes shy about. Right?

Edgar: Yes. That, rather than saying hello to those things, I didn't say anything at all—so that I wouldn't have to say good-bye. Like standing in place with all those things still around anyhow.

Pastor: That's right. And those things still wanted something from you. Your daughters, grandchildren, and work. And of course Madge, who wasn't far away and, in fact, wanted more of your time after the girls went off on their own.

Edgar: And there I was stuck, or more like letting myself get stuck, and still people—I mean Madge and the guys at work, bowling, and even Joe Paterno—expecting something from me.

Pastor: What you saw as something to dread, others saw as an opportunity, and you got depressed over it all.

Edgar: Yes, depression is the word for it, I guess.

Pastor: So that is what we worked on. The dilemma of saying hello and good-bye to all those things. Each time we got together we talked about that, not only how that happened to you in the past, say with your father and mother, but also how it happened to you in the here and now with bowling, work, and with Madge. We even talked about it in terms of our own relationship, didn't we?

Edgar: Yeah, I remember that clearly. I think that it was about session six—or was it five?—I don't remember. I was mad at you because you kept saying that we only had a few sessions left, and I really didn't like that. (Silence for a few moments) I was mad, but then you started talking about hello and good-bye again.

Pastor: I remember that, too. It seemed clear to both of us that hello and good-bye had something to do with our relationship, too.

Edgar: It seemed embarrassing at the time.

Pastor: Embarrassing?

Edgar: Yeah. Like I couldn't just rush into my shell because there you were talking about all that stuff, and it had something to do with us. It was like you said at the time—nowhere to hide because there was the two of us, and you wanted to deal with it.

Pastor: Yeah, and it really was an important session, wasn't it?

Edgar: I found out that, just like Joe Lewis said, you can run but you can't hide. I found out that I was missing so much, and maybe even hurting people by trying to avoid them. I guess that is what was embarrassing. I was protecting myself from good-bye—even though there is always a good-bye—and losing out on so much of the hellos.

Pastor: That was a big breakthrough for us both. From that we talked about all the other ways you had done the same thing and how you started seeing the way that it worked before it got out of hand. You started catching yourself avoiding the good times for fear of them ending.

Edgar: Not that it was stupid, but that it left me alone when I wasn't alone. Well, maybe stupid is the right word.

Pastor: Stupid may be too strong of a word, Edgar; more like outdated.

Edgar: I remember you talking about that. Doing that may have worked when I was a kid but not when I am an adult and a grandfather!

Pastor: Right! (Beth and Edgar continue talking about the FRP and how it was discussed in the three fields, as well as how Edgar began to have more and more ability to see it in play and how he began to have some mastery over it. This review of the nine sessions continues until the following conversation takes place.)

Pastor: Well, Edgar, it seems that you have a pretty good handle on things. The old hello and good-bye may raise its head again, but it seems that you will have the ability to see it coming and do something about it.

Edgar: I don't think that it will always be out of my life, but I sure know that avoiding the hello isn't worth it just because things change.

Pastor: Good. There is something I want to bring up to you that might be helpful if you think so.

Edgar: What's that?

Pastor: If you would like, why don't you give me a call in three months, say at the end of July, and we can get together for an hour and see how things are going as far as hello and good-bye is concerned. Sort of like a check-up to see how you are doing with it. I think that by then you should have things pretty much in sight.

Edgar: You mean we may get together and talk about it some more?

Pastor: Well, for one more time just to see how things are going. If it seems that you want to discuss the hello and good-bye or something else, then I think we could talk about you going to see one of the people at the pastoral counseling center at the Methodist church. If you would like, let's get together, but that is up to you.

Edgar: Only if I want to.

Pastor: Yes, only if you would like to report on how it is going with hello and good-bye.

Edgar: O.K. I'll remember that . . . end of July would be about three months.

Pastor: Yeah, of course I'll see you here at church and around town. Maybe not so much at the bowling alley. I think I'm going to be banned from that place.

Edgar: Not if I have anything to say about it. Say, is there anything more I can do at the church? Madge and I thought that we might volunteer at the food bank. Let me know if there is anything else I can do.

Pastor: You better mean that, buster, because you will be getting a call soon if you do!

Edgar: I mean it. By the way, there were some folks talking about the new hymnal in the last Sunday school class led by Bill Morris. What do you think about some of the new hymns that are replacing some of the old ones?

Pastor: Is this hello and good-bye again?

Edgar: Well, maybe, but some of our favorites are missing, and it is not clear to me why that is so.

Pastor: I'm confused about some of it, too, but the reason the church is looking at the hymns is because . . . (The conversation continues with social leave-taking and ends.) Well, Edgar, our time is up. It has been a real pleasure seeing you in these sessions. I have learned a lot, and I appreciate the opportunity we have had together.

Edgar: Thank you, Beth. I'll see you next Sunday . . . beat Pitt!

Pastor: Beat Pitt!

Conclusion

The sessions didn't really end for either Beth or Edgar with the Penn State benediction. Beth found herself continuing to review the course of the counseling and found herself with mixed feelings: mostly satisfaction with a little bit of sadness. Though her relationship with Edgar would continue in many ways, the ending of the counseling marked a developmental closing of part of their relationship. She could safely assume that Edgar had similar feelings and that future contacts with him would, though in different contexts than the counseling context, be different. These feelings, Beth noted, were things to be discussed in her next peer group supervision. For Edgar the repetitive evaluation of the FRP during the counseling process would be carried with him as he became his own counselor, and not only would he benefit from the process but so would those who cared for and were cared for by him.

This book began with a rather simple thesis: people come to pastors for help with their personal problems, and pastors can go to people to offer help. This very fact, however, is bounded by an important anthropological and pragmatic concern, and that is the concern with time. As finite creatures we have only so much of it. This is so in terms of our life on this earth as living creatures in relationships and in terms of the amount of time we have to devote to any particular task. There is only so much time in the day, month, and year for all that we are called to do in our finite private and public lives. This thesis is further buttressed by two basic assumptions about pastoral counseling. Pastoral counseling helps people help themselves, and pastoral counseling gives the pastor, as theologian, the raw material for theological reflection.

Time-limited pastoral counseling is one response to

the thesis and the assumptions incorporated in the thesis. It answers the pragmatic concern of the limited amount of time that pastors and parishioners have to deal with personal problems, while taking seriously our responsibilities in the limited amount of time we each have as stewards of God's creation. Pastoral counseling, whether it is time-limited or open-ended, is basically training for and the development of ethical living in relationships. In time-limited pastoral counseling the boundaries of our ethical responsibilities are underscored. Our relationships are radically bounded by our limited temporality. According to the Old Testament theologian Claus Westermann, human temporal limitation and human ethical responsibility are a major part of the anthropology presented in Genesis 1–11. Genesis is much more than the creation stories, for it also includes human limitation. In blessing, one receives from one's creator the capacity for propagation; this includes, however, that people are bound to a short span of existence. One exists as a person only in the span which leads from birth to death.[3] Our hopes and our fears are boiling in the crucible of our temporality. The question, then, is how best can we live with this fact, for God calls us to do just that.

Beth's work with Edgar in a time-limited counseling contract dealt with the ethical problem of living in relationships. Through the investigation of the FRP of hello and good-bye, the two of them were able to investigate Edgar's—and all of our—fears and hopes for human relationships and for all of creation. In Edgar's case the fear and the hope almost seemed to cancel each other out, resulting in Edgar's description of being sluggish and standing in place. Yet the clock was always running. Through the counseling relationship, Edgar was confronted by Beth with how this paralyzing situation was apparent in his past and in his current relationships, including the relationship with his pastor. In a sense Edgar was much like Jacob before his wrestling match with the angel, though without all the wheeling and dealing of the patriarch. Rather than asking for and receiving the blessing, he had tried to control all for himself. This was a project that was doomed to failure. Like Jacob, he found himself alone at night unable to sleep. In a sense the counseling was Edgar's wrestling match in which he needed to come to grips with his destiny and receive God's blessing. Then he could face his relationships, open handed, with the noticeable limp of Jacob that marks all of us fallible and limited creatures.[4]

If the counseling is helpful, then only one goal of pastoral counseling is completed. The second goal is an ongoing one and is one fulfilled by Beth and every pastoral counselor. To completely fulfill the vocation of pastoral counseling, the counselor must also be a pastoral theologian. To be a theologian is to declare publicly what it is to be fully human in the face of a loving creator God who has made God's self manifest in history and through the incarnation. For the pastoral theologian this means not only the solitary study of scripture, tradition, and the living human document (to borrow from Boisen), but also the public declaration of faith seeking understanding in the context of the community. This is executed through the pastor's supervision, either in individual or group supervision, and in the pastor's preaching, teaching, and administration of church programs.

Beth learned much about the human condition in her work with Edgar. Being a student of the theological tradition, she was aware of what the theologians and the scriptures tell us about our limited freedom. She had read and incorporated what theologians such as

Westermann, Barth, Soelle, Boff, Fiorenza, and the Niebuhrs have told us about the ethical implications of temporality. She also had read those from the human sciences that further clarified for her the human condition. Gustafson, Mann, Gilligan, and Nagy all proved to be helpful. Other pastoral theologians, such as Patton, Gerkin, and Hiltner, also made a contribution to some of her theological and anthropological assumptions as she approached her counseling with people in need.

Finally, though, she was confronted with all of this in the context of that which was empirical and that which was experienced. She was in relationship with another human struggling with the issues at hand. She was in relationship with Edgar. What she had studied and understood in general was confronted with the particular of the counseling relationship. This confrontation provided for her, and provides for every pastoral theologian, the grist for the theological mill from which theological articulation results, albeit as provisional and tentative as that articulation may be. Every pastoral counselor is called to help people help themselves. In addition, he or she needs to reflect on this helping process and enunciate clearly what this means about the human condition and the human obligation before God. Time-limited pastoral counseling in the parish affords the pastor both the rationale and the structure for attaining these goals. The issues will be different with each counseling relationship. Hello and good-bye could be replaced by hello with no good-bye (delayed grief); good-bye with no hello (social isolation and depression); anger and remorse (displacement and shame); and many others limited only by the time we have to be in the relationship of service and care, as well as to be served and cared for.

Notes

1. Luborsky, *Principles of Psychoanalytic Psychotherapy, A Manual for Supportive-Expressive Treatment* (New York: Basic Books, 1989), p. 143.
2. For a detailed discussion of this issue as well as other issues in termination see Luborsky, *Principles of Psychoanalytic Psychotherapy,* chapter 9.
3. Claus Westermann, *Elements of Old Testament Theology* (Atlanta: John Knox Press, 1982), p. 103.
4. My thanks to Brad Binau, Ph.D., a pastor at La Jolla Lutheran Church in La Jolla, California, for some of these images. Pastor Binau has wrestled himself with Genesis 32:22-30 in a series of sermons entitled "Coming to Grips" that he has shared with me over the past four years in personal correspondence.

Appendix A

Critical Criteria for Short-term Counseling
(Chapter 2)

1. Is there a clear presenting problem in terms of a Focal Relational Problem (FRP)?
2. Is there give-and-take in the interview and evidence of a meaningful relationship in the counselee's past—particularly during early childhood?
3. Is there a capacity on the counselee's part to relate flexibly with the pastor during the interview?
4. Is there a psychological mindedness on the part of the counselee?
5. Is there a motivation for change?

The pastor should have a positive response to all five of these criteria for the proper selection of a candidate for short-term counseling. If there is any hesitation a consultation or referral should be considered (chapter 4).

Appendix B

The Pastoral Diagnostic Interview
(Chapter 3)

The following is an outline of the process of the diagnostic interview. The pastor should not allow the outline of the interview to inhibit the process. Rather, the pastor should use this outline as a reference to guide the process of gleaning critical information necessary in assessing the needs of the counselee, and the suitability of time-limited counseling in addressing the need.

Joining (5 minutes)
1. Making personal contact
2. More than small-talk
3. Sharing things in common
4. First impressions noted

Presenting Problem (15 minutes)
1. "What brings you to speak to me at this time?"
2. Counselee uses his/her own words
3. Clarifying and sharpening the issue through dialogue

History Taking (15 minutes)
1. Family history
2. Educational background
3. Work background

4. Medical problems, medications, and alcohol and drug abuse
5. Meaningful relationships inside and outside the family

Previous Help (10 minutes)
1. Attempts at self-help
2. Professional help

Religious or Theological Issues (10-15 minutes)
1. Religious background
2. Church involvement
3. Ideas about relationship with God/Christ/Holy Spirit

Conclusion (10 minutes)
1. Review of the presenting problem
2. Begin to develop language for a Focal Relational Problem (FRP)
3. Confirm the FRP in dialogue with the counselee

At the conclusion of the diagnostic interview the pastor should offer another interview for further discussion, for consultation, or a contract should be offered for time-limited counseling if the critical criteria for time-limited counseling are met.

Index

Index